RECIPES
·FROM THE·
MICRO
BREWERIES
·OF AMERICA·

RECIPES
·FROM THE·
MICRO
BREWERIES
·OF AMERICA·

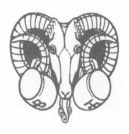

By
Leslie Mansfield

CELESTIALARTS
Berkeley, Toronto

CELESTIALARTS

P.O. Box 7123
Berkeley, California 94707

Distributed in Canada by Ten Speed Canada, in the United Kingdom and Europe by Airlift Books, in New Zealand by Southern Publishers Group, in Australia by Simon & Schuster Australia, in South Africa by Real Books, and in Singapore, Malaysia, Hong Kong, and Thailand by Berkeley Books.

Cover and interior design by Greene Design
Cover photograph by Larry Kunkel
Photo styling by Veronica Randall
Public Domain Art thanks to Dover Publications

Library of Congress Card Catalog Number on file with the publisher

First printing, 2001
Printed in the United States

1 2 3 4 5 6 7 — 05 04 03 02 01

To my wonderful husband, Richard Mansfield,
whose invaluable and patient coaching
has taught me the difference between
bock and a stout.

Acknowledgements

Deepest gratitude goes to my husband, Richard Mansfield, who has helped me with every step—his name belongs on the title page along with mine. To my wonderful parents, Stewart and Marcia Whipple, who have taught me perseverance. To my publisher, Phil Wood, who makes dreams a reality. To my dear friend and editor, Veronica Randall, who was always there for me in every way, especially when I needed her the most. To Mark Anderson, who had the vision for this book. To Tom Dalldorf and his *Celebrator Beer News*, for his invaluable assistance in the project. To Victoria Randall, for her invaluable assistance and eagle eyes. To Brad Greene, the most creative book designer in the world. To Larry Kunkel, for his beautiful cover photography.

Table of Contents

Forward

Although the microbrewing industry in America is barely twenty-five-years old (and the brewpub phenomenon is younger still), today's beer lovers are a knowledgeable and enthusiastic group, schooled in beer styles and confident in beery preferences. But the American "good beer" movement is in its infancy when contrasted with the extensive history of the European craft brewing tradition.

Beer is as old as civilization itself, having begun with the transition of nomadic tribes to an agriculture-based society. These people put down roots (so to speak) primarily to grow wheat and barley for the production of bread and, as Professor Solomon Katz of the University of Pennsylvania suggests, beer. From its beginnings in the Tigris-Euphrates Valley to fueling construction of the pyramids, beer has been a part of the rise and development of civilization for several thousand years.

Because the process of making beer requires heating the water in which the malt is steeped, beer has also been credited with reducing sickness and death caused by bacteria-laden drinking water, as well as advancing the growth of mankind itself. The ancient convention of drinking beer with meals (including breakfast) was born of necessity—drinking water made you sick, while drinking beer did not. It wasn't until Louis Pasteur discovered the world of microorganisms in the late eighteenth century that we learned the cause of this phenomenon.

Beer, then, has a long history, especially at mealtimes in Germany and the Czech Republic. The rich English pub tradition is based on food and beer. The Belgian experience takes it to another level altogether: Exotic, complex, spontaneously fermented sour beers are married with rich, equally exotic dishes, some of which are prepared with the same beer that is served with the meal. Belgian beer is rarely enjoyed without food accompaniment.

The evolution of beer drinking in America goes back to the first Colonists. The Pilgrims actually stopped at Plymouth Rock because the ship on which they had booked passage to Virginia ran out of beer.

Early immigrants to America brought their beer-making traditions with them. Germans settled in the Midwest and made beer—the beers that made Milwaukee famous! By the start of the twentieth century, over four thousand breweries were in production making a wide variety of beers— mostly European-style lagers. Production was local, and distribution went only as far as a horse-drawn wagon could deliver. There was no refrigeration, and beer is very perishable.

Our great experiment with social engineering called Prohibition lasted from 1919 to 1933 and served to strangle the brewing industry. Few breweries were able to successfully reopen after repeal of the Volstead Act.

Beer went to war in WWII, and returning servicemen brought with them a taste for lighter, more carbonated (adjunct) lager beer. Postwar mass-marketing and advertising, along with improved transportation and refrigeration, eliminated a lot of competition and resulted in a greatly reduced choice of brewing products. Indeed, there were fewer than sixty breweries operating in the United States by the mid-1960s.

International travel and a rebirth of home-brewing by that time stimulated in some people a taste for real beer (all-malt brewing). Anchor Brewing Company in San Francisco reintroduced all-malt brewing to America in the mid-1960s when the Beatles were topping the music charts. The first American microbrewery, New Albion, was established in Sonoma County, California, in 1977. The first brewpub in the United States was Grant's Yakima Brewing and Malting Company in Washington state in 1982. Mendocino Brewing Company was the first brewpub to open in California in August 1983. Real beer had gained a foothold and was not to be denied.

In less than a quarter-century, brewing in America has exploded, giving every region in the country its own coterie of breweries making fresh, characterful, richly flavored beers for local or regional consumption.

Sophisticated "foodies" are well versed in gourmet cooking, the latest trend in restaurants, and the most recent twist on food and wine pairings, but few have yet to experience the gustatorial delights of great food served with great beer. Veteran cookbook author Leslie Mansfield redresses that glaring error. Leslie and I have gone to the very best of America's small or regional breweries in search of their favorite recipes that showcase food and the art of brewing.

Read, taste, and enjoy the product of the extensive research, formulation, tastings, and criticism contained in this compendium of beery gustatory excess. And what good cook would be without a glass of good beer while creating the recipes within?

Cheers,
Tom Dalldorf

Tom Dalldorf is editor/publisher of the *Celebrator Beer News* and a longtime food, wine, and beer enthusiast.

Glossary of Beer and Brewing Terms

adjunct: Fermentable matter other than barley malt used to make beer lighter or cheaper (rice, corn, corn syrup).

ale: An ancient style of beer made with naturally occurring ale yeast, which ferments at the top of the wort. Ales are generally not aged as long as lagers.

barley: The primary ingredient in beer (after water). Sprouted barley is kilned at high temperatures to become malt. Darker malt makes darker beer.

barrel: The term used to measure brewery output; equal to 31 U.S. gallons.

beer: A fermented drink made mainly from malted grain and usually seasoned (bittered) with hops.

bottle-conditioning: Secondary or refermentation in the bottle similar to champagne production, producing a finer, more complex product.

brewpub: A tavern or restaurant that brews its own beer for sale with food. Some states allow brewpubs to distribute beer to other retailers.

BU: Bitterness Units, or International Bitterness Units (IBU), measures the amount of bitterness in a beer, usually from hops.

cask-conditioning: Secondary fermentation and maturation in the cask; the beer is then served from the cask by gravity or a handpump.

dry-hopping: The addition of hops after the boil,

usually in fermentation, giving additional aroma and some bittering.

fruit beer: Any style of beer made with fruit.

helles: German for "pale"; usually a pale yellow lager.

hops: The cone-shaped flowers of the female hop plant used to flavor, bitter, and preserve beer.

kraeusening: Adding unfermented wort to finished beer to develop natural carbonation in the brewing process.

lager: The style of beer made with lager yeast, which ferments at the bottom of the wort and is aged (lagered) for an extended time at cold temperatures.

lauter: Running off the wort from the mash tun (from the German word for "to clarify".)

malt: Grain (usually barley) that has been "malted" (allowed to sprout) to develop maltose sugars that are converted by yeast cells, producing alcohol and carbon dioxide.

mash tun: The vessel used to extract malt sugars from grain by soaking in hot water.

Oktoberfest: A 16-day festival in Germany beginning in late September. Many smaller Oktoberfests are celebrated in other parts of the world. Also a beer style (see maerzen).

original gravity: The measurement of the density of fermentable sugars in the mash, which affects the amount of alcohol in the beer.

pasteurization: The process of heating of beer to kill microbes that can cause spoilage.

Reinheitsgebot: The German beer purity law of 1516 stated that beer would be made with only malted grains, yeast, hops, and water.

session beer: A malty, English-style ale, usually of lower alcohol content.

wort: The sweet liquid produced by cooking or "mashing" malted barley and other grains. Yeast then converts the wort to beer through fermentation.

yeast: A single-celled microorganism that consumes sugars and converts them into alcohol and carbon dioxide. Beer is made with either top-fermenting ale yeast or bottom-fermenting lager yeast.

Common Beer Styles

Abbey beers: Beers produced by or for religious orders in Belgium, other than Trappist beers. A style of Belgian beer. Example: Abbey of Leffe.

altbier: German for "old beer." A copper-colored German ale now scarce in the land of lager. Example: Widmer Altbier.

barley wine: A very strong ale, 8-11% alcohol by volume, suitable for extended aging. Example: Anchor Old Foghorn.

bitter: A British-style ale with a pronounced hop character. Example: Young's Bitter.

bock: A strong, usually dark German lager traditionally featured in spring. Example: Einbecker Hell Bock.

brown ale: A mild, malty brown beer associated with England and Scotland. Example: Scottish & Newcastle Brown Ale.

doppelbock: German for "double bock." An extra-strong dark version of bock beer. Example: Ayinger Celebrator.

dunkel: German for "dark." Any dark beer—usually a lager. Example: Aventinus Weizen Doppelbock.

export: A German lager usually drier and less hoppy than most pilsners. Example: Dortmunder Actien Brauerei (DAB) Export.

framboise: A Belgian-style lambic beer made with raspberries. Example: Lindemans Framboise.

imperial stout: A very strong stout, 7-10% alcohol by volume. Example: North Coast Brewing's Imperial Stout.

India pale ale: A strong, bitter beer originally brewed in Britain for export to soldiers in India and now favored by Pacific Coast beer enthusiasts. Example: BridgePort Brewing's IPA.

koelsch: A light, delicate, golden ale associated with Cologne, a city in Germany. Example: P.J. Frueh Koelsch.

kriek: A Belgian lambic beer made with cherries. Example: Boon Kriek Lambic.

lambic: A Belgian ale low in carbonation that is traditionally fermented only with wild yeast. Example: Cantillon Gueuze-Lambic.

maibock: German for "May bock." A strong, pale beer brewed in the fall and traditionally enjoyed in the spring. Example: Gordon Biersch Maibock.

maerzen: German for "March." A medium to strong, malty beer brewed in March for consumption at fall celebrations such as Germany's Oktoberfest. Example: Ayinger Oktober Fest-Maerzen.

mild: An amber, malty English-style ale usually of lower alcohol content. A "session" beer. Example: Highgate Mild.

Oktoberfest: See maerzen.

old ale: British term for a medium-strong, dark ale consumed in winter. Example: Adnams Old Ale.

pale ale: A fruity, estery, milder version of India pale ale. Example: Sierra Nevada Pale Ale.

pilsner/pilsener/pils: A crisp, pale, hoppy lager. Example: Pilsner Urquell.

porter: A dark ale first brewed in eighteenth-century London, made popular by the "porters," who were the day laborers of the time. Example: Deschutes Black Butte Porter.

rauchbier: A smoky-flavored lager developed in Germany that is made by wood-smoking the malt. Example: Aecht Schlenkerla Rauchbier.

saison: A mildly sour, traditional Belgian summer ale flavored with spices or herbs. Example: Saison Dupont.

Scotch ale: A rich, malty, copper-colored strong ale originally made in Scotland. Example: Gordon Highland Scotch Ale.

steam beer: A unique beer made with lager yeast at top-fermenting ale temperatures in shallow "cool ships" during gold rush days in San Francisco; now made only by Anchor Brewing Company.

stout: A richly malty or dry black beer. Example: Guinness Stout.

Trappist ale: A strong, fruity ale made by Trappist monks in Belgium. Example: Chimay Grand Reserve.

Vienna: A reddish, sweet, malty lager originally made in Vienna. Example: Samuel Adams Boston Lager.

weizenbier: German for "wheat beer." Any beer between 20% and 60% wheat, usually filtered (clear). Example: Erdinger Weissbier.

wheat beer: See weizenbier.

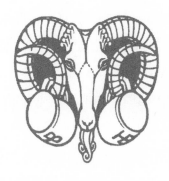

Alaskan Brewing Company

In 1986 the great state of Alaska was blessed by the arrival of one of America's premier microbreweries, the Alaskan Brewing Company. It became the 67th operating brewery in the United States and the only one in Alaska. Since that time their beers have brought fame and glory to the northernmost state by winning more than 25 major medals and awards, including "Best Beer in the Nation" in the 1988 Great American Beer Festival Consumer Preference Poll. Mush to the north, chase a polar bear, gaze at the northern lights, and suck down a cool one in the true land of cool.

Amber Crab-Stuffed Mushrooms

*These aren't just for mucklukers, no way.
Hearty enough to serve on the Iditarod Trail
and soul-satisfying enough for the Superbowl.
Make plenty.*

40 large mushrooms

2 tablespoons butter

2 tablespoons minced garlic

1 tablespoon dried parsley

1 1/2 teaspoons rosemary, crumbled

1 cup Alaskan Brewing Company Amber Ale

1 tablespoon Worcestershire sauce

1 teaspoon freshly ground black pepper

8 ounces cream cheese, softened

1/4 cup dry bread crumbs

3 cups cooked Alaskan crabmeat,
    picked through for shells

1 cup Asiago cheese, grated

1 cup kasseri cheese, grated

(continued on next page)

Preheat oven to 375 degrees F.

Remove the stems from the mushrooms, chop and set aside. Place the caps on a rimmed baking sheet.

In a skillet, melt the butter over medium heat. Add garlic, parsley, and rosemary and sauté until fragrant. Add the chopped mushroom stems and sauté until liquid evaporates. Stir in the ale, Worcestershire sauce, and black pepper, reduce heat to low, and simmer for 10 minutes. Transfer mixture to a large bowl. Stir in the cream cheese and bread crumbs until blended. Stir in the crabmeat. With a small spoon, fill the mushrooms caps with the crab-mushroom mixture. Bake for 20 minutes. Remove from the oven and top with the grated cheeses. Return to the oven and bake an additional 5 to 10 minutes, or until the cheese is bubbly.

Serves 8 to 10

 Serve with
Alaskan Brewing Company Amber Ale

Crab Lasagna

Tony Hand created this most luscious lasagna. Crusty, hot garlic bread and a tossed green salad make a complete, memorable meal.

Crab Filling:

2 tablespoons butter

2 tablespoons all-purpose flour

1 cup heavy cream

1 cup milk

$1/2$ cup minced onion

2 tablespoons Alaskan Brewing Company Pale Ale

2 cloves garlic, minced

$1/2$ teaspoon freshly ground black pepper

$1/8$ teaspoon nutmeg

1 pound cooked Alaskan Dungeness crabmeat

2 cups lightly steamed broccoli florets

8 ounces lasagna noodles

8 ounces mozzarella cheese, shredded

4 ounces freshly grated Parmesan cheese

4 ounces freshly grated Romano cheese

$1/2$ cup pine nuts

(continued on next page)

3

Preheat oven to 350 degrees F. Lightly oil a 9 x 9-inch baking dish.

For the filling: In a large saucepan, melt the butter over medium heat. Whisk in the flour and cook until bubbly. Whisk in the cream and milk until smooth. Whisk in the onion, ale, garlic, pepper, and nutmeg. Lower heat to a simmer, and, whisking constantly, continue to cook until slightly thickened. Stir in the crab and broccoli. Remove from heat and set aside.

Bring a large pot of salted water to a boil. Add the lasagna to the water and cook for about 8 minutes. Do not overcook or the pasta will be difficult to handle. Drain well.

Layer half the lasagna sheets in the bottom of the prepared baking dish, overlapping the pieces to cover bottom completely. Spread half of the filling mixture evenly over the pasta.

Cover filling with half of the mozzarella, Parmesan, Romano, and pine nuts. Layer the remaining pasta over the cheeses. Spread the remaining filling over the pasta. Top with the remaining cheeses and pine nuts. Bake for about 55 minutes, or until bubbly and the top is golden brown.

Serves 4

 **Serve with**

Alaskan Brewing Company Pale Ale

Fill with mingled cream and amber,
I will drain that glass again.
Such hilarious visions clamber
Through the chambers of my brain.
Quaintest thoughts–queerest fancies,
Come to life and fade away:
What care I how time advances?
I am drinking ale today.

Edgar Allan Poe

Spinach and Mozzarella Salad
WITH ALASKAN ESB DRESSING

If you can't get your greens from Alaska's famous Matanuska Valley, then head to your local supermarket for the ingredients to this great summer salad.

$1/2$ cup olive oil

$1/4$ cup Alaskan Brewing Company ESB, at room temperature

2 tablespoons balsamic vinegar

2 cloves garlic, minced

1 teaspoon basil

$1/4$ teaspoon lemon pepper

$1/4$ teaspoon salt

8 ounces mozzarella cut into $1/4$-inch cubes

10 ounces baby spinach

1 small red onion, thinly sliced

3 Mandarin oranges, sectioned

In a large bowl, whisk together the olive oil, beer, vinegar, garlic, basil, lemon pepper, and salt. Add the mozzarella, cover, and let stand 3 hours at room temperature.

Add the baby spinach to the dressing and toss to coat. Divide the salad onto 6 plates. Distribute the red onion slices and Mandarin orange sections on top of the salads.

Serves 6

 **Serve with**

Alaskan Brewing Company ESB

Fiery Pale Ale Prawns

Celebrate the bounty of the cold waters of the Great North by making this easy, fantastic dish. Crack a cold one, invite some friends, and fire up the barbie.

$2/3$ cup Alaskan Brewing Company Pale Ale

$1/3$ cup honey

3 tablespoons cornstarch

1 clove garlic, minced

$1/4$ teaspoon cayenne

$3^{1}/2$ pounds fresh Alaskan spot prawns,
   or other medium-sized shrimp,
   shelled with tails left on

In a shallow bowl, whisk together the ale, honey, cornstarch, garlic, and cayenne until smooth. Add the prawns and toss to coat. Cover and chill in the refrigerator for at least 6 hours, or overnight, stirring several times as they marinate.

Prepare the grill. Remove prawns from the marinade and thread onto skewers. Place the prawns over hot coals and cook, turning once, until done, about 3 minutes each side.

Serves 6 to 8

 Serve with

Alaskan Brewing Company Pale Ale

Stout and Ginger Pudding

The Alaskan Brewing Company's Ken and MaryAnn Vaughn serve up this cozy, steamed pudding to their grateful guests when the weather turns cold.

$1^1/2$ cups brown sugar

$2/3$ cup butter, softened

3 eggs

$2^1/2$ cups all-purpose flour

2 teaspoons ground ginger

$1^1/2$ teaspoons baking powder

1 teaspoon cinnamon

$1/4$ teaspoon nutmeg

$1^1/2$ cups Alaskan Brewing Company Stout

1 cup chopped candied ginger

1 cup golden raisins

1 cup chopped walnuts

Butter and flour a 1^1/$_2$-quart pudding mold with a tight-fitting lid.

In a large bowl, cream the brown sugar and butter together until light and fluffy. Add the eggs, one at a time, beating well after each addition.

In a separate bowl, sift together flour, ground ginger, baking powder, cinnamon, and nutmeg. Add the flour mixture to the creamed mixture alternately with the stout by thirds. Gently fold in the candied ginger, raisins, and walnuts. Spoon batter into prepared pudding mold and fasten the lid.

Place a steamer rack in a large kettle and set the mold on the rack. Add enough water to reach two-thirds of the way up the sides of the mold. Cover tightly and bring to a boil. Reduce heat to medium-low and steam for 1^1/$_2$ hours, checking occasionally to make certain that the water is

(continued on next page)

simmering and adding more water if necessary. Remove from kettle and let cool.

To serve, unmold onto a serving plate. Serve warm or cold.

Serves 12 to 16

 **Serve with**
Alaskan Brewing Company Stout

> *'Did you ever taste beer?'*
> *'I had a sip of it once,'*
> *said the small servant.*
> *'Here's a state of things!'*
> *cried Mr. Swiveller . . .*
> *'She never tasted it—it can't be tasted*
> *in a sip!'*

Charles Dickens,
Ye Olde Curiosity Shop

Anchor Brewing Company

In 1965, when Fritz Maytag purchased the old Anchor brewery, nobody could guess that he was setting in motion a series of events that would launch America's microbrewery revolution. His flagship Anchor Steam Beer™ quickly became a nation-wide favorite with craft beer lovers and helped to inspire budding brewers to open their own microbreweries. Beer lovers everywhere owe a great debt of thanks to this great and influential pioneer and leader of the craft beer movement.

Lamb Shanks Braised in Liberty Ale

Philip Rogers dug deeply into his repertoire of great recipes to find us this winter gem. Not for your friends who are eating light—this extra hearty dish will satisfy even the heartiest appetites.

1/4 cup olive oil

4 lamb shanks

Salt and freshly ground black pepper, to taste

1 onion, chopped

3 carrots, sliced

2 ribs celery, chopped

3 cloves garlic, minced

2 cups Anchor Steam Brewing Company Liberty Ale

2 cups chopped tomatoes

1 tablespoon tomato paste

1 teaspoon rosemary

1 teaspoon thyme

Preheat oven to 375 degrees F.

In a large pot, heat the olive oil over medium-high heat. Season the lamb shanks with salt and pepper and add to the pot. Brown well on all sides. Transfer lamb shanks to a plate and set aside. Add the onion, carrots, and celery to the pot and sauté until the onion is translucent. Add the garlic and sauté until fragrant. Stir in the ale and lower heat to a simmer. Stir in the tomatoes, tomato paste, rosemary, and thyme. Return lamb shanks to the pot and bring to a simmer. Cover pot and transfer to the oven. Bake for about 2$1/2$ to 3 hours, or until lamb is very tender. Add more ale during cooking if it gets too dry.

Serves 6

 Serve with Anchor Liberty Ale

Wheat Beer Sorbet

You will need an ice cream maker to make David Stevenson's stunning and really different sorbet.

3 cups Anchor Steam Brewing Company Wheat Beer

$1^3/4$ cups sugar

$1^1/2$ cups water

$1/4$ cup freshly squeezed lemon juice

$1/4$ cup freshly squeezed lime juice

$1/8$ teaspoon salt

In a large saucepan, add the beer and bring to a simmer over medium heat. Watch constantly because the beer will foam over as the alcohol is boiled off. If it begins to foam over, remove from heat until it subsides. Reduce heat to medium-low and continue to simmer for about 5 minutes, or until it is no longer foamy. Stir in the sugar, water, lemon juice, lime juice, and salt and increase heat to medium. Simmer until sugar dissolves. Remove from heat and let cool. Cover and chill thoroughly in the refrigerator.

Pour into ice cream maker and process according to manufacturer's instructions. In the unlikely event that you have any left over, store in the freezer.

Makes about 1 1/2 quarts

 Serve with Anchor Wheat Beer

Stout Black Forest Cheesecake

Chocolate and stout—a match made in brewer's heaven! Really! You have to try it.

Crust:

2$\frac{1}{2}$ cups chocolate graham cracker crumbs

$\frac{1}{4}$ cup sugar

$\frac{2}{3}$ cup melted butter

3 tablespoons Anchor Steam Brewing Company Stout

Filling:

1 cup semisweet chocolate chips

$\frac{2}{3}$ cup Anchor Steam Brewing Company Stout

24 ounces cream cheese, softened

$\frac{3}{4}$ cup sugar

5 tablespoons cornstarch

3 eggs

1 egg yolk

2 teaspoons vanilla extract

$\frac{2}{3}$ cup chopped Bing cherries

Preheat oven to 325 degrees F.

For the crust: In the bowl of a food processor, combine the graham cracker crumbs and sugar and pulse until smooth. Add the melted butter and stout and pulse to blend. Press the mixture into the bottom of a 10-inch springform pan.

For the filling: In the top of a double boiler, combine chocolate chips and stout. Melt together over barely simmering water. Set aside and let cool.

In a large bowl, beat the cream cheese, sugar, and cornstarch together until smooth, scraping the sides often. Add the eggs, one at a time, beating well after each addition. Add the egg yolk and vanilla and beat until smooth. Stir in the reserved chocolate mixture and cherries. Pour batter into the prepared crust and place springform pan on a baking sheet. Bake for

(continued on next page)

about 1 hour, or until cheesecake is very lightly golden and begins to pull away from the sides of the pan. Cool to room temperature, then cover and chill overnight.

Serves 12

 **Serve with Anchor Stout**

Back and side go bare, go bare,
Both foot and hand go cold;
But, belly, God send thee good
ale enough,
Whether it be new or old.

Bishop Still (John)

Anderson Valley Brewing Company

Who'd guess that in a remote valley in Mendocino, in the town of Boonville where old-timers speak a linguistically unique dialect of English known as "Boontling," you would find one of America's great microbreweries. Founded in the early 1980s by Kenneth and Kimberley Allen, the Anderson Valley Brewing Company has racked up an impressive array of medals and accolades for their beers. Visit the brewery, and hoist a beer to the best of the Anderson Valley.

Wild Greens with Ginger AND Hoppy Pale Ale Dressing

If you cannot find a source for wild greens, select a mixture of bib, butter, and romaine for this salad.

1/3 cup Anderson Valley Brewing Company Poleeko Gold Pale Ale

2 tablespoons finely minced fresh ginger

2 tablespoons honey

2 tablespoons chopped red onion

2 tablespoons sesame oil

1 tablespoon balsamic vinegar

1/2 teaspoon Dijon mustard

1/2 teaspoon salt

1/4 teaspoon freshly ground black pepper

3/4 cup vegetable oil

6 cups mixed wild greens

In a large bowl, whisk together the ale, ginger, honey, red onion, sesame oil, balsamic vinegar, Dijon mustard, salt, and pepper until smooth. Add the vegetable oil in a thin stream, whisking constantly, until everything is thoroughly incorporated. Add the greens and toss with the dressing and divide onto 6 plates.

Serves 6

Serve with Anderson Valley Brewing Company Boont Amber Ale

Lentil and Stout Soup

A dish of these savory lentils will drive the coastal rain and fog from your body and soul.

2 tablespoons olive oil

1 onion, chopped

2 carrots, sliced

5 cloves garlic, minced

3 cups Anderson Valley Brewing Company
   Barney Flats Stout

2 cups green lentils

1 cup chicken stock

Salt and freshly ground black pepper, to taste

In a large pot, heat the olive oil over medium heat. Add the onion, carrots, and garlic and sauté until tender. Stir in the stout and lower heat to a simmer. Stir in the lentils and chicken stock and continue to simmer over medium-low heat, stirring often, until lentils are very tender, about 30 minutes. Season with salt and pepper and serve immediately.

Serves 6

Serve with Anderson Valley Brewing Company High Roller Wheat Beer

I would give all my fame for a pot of ale and safety.

William Shakespeare, *King Henry V*

Stout-Brined Smoked Venison

Stout and venison are a great combination. But this brine works well with beef or pork, too.

1½ cups Anderson Valley Brewing Company Barney Flats Stout

½ cup non-iodized salt

¼ cup honey

¼ cup minced onions

1 tablespoon Worcestershire sauce

1 clove garlic, minced

1½ teaspoons Tabasco sauce

2 bay leaves

½ teaspoon freshly ground black pepper

½ teaspoon chili powder

½ teaspoon marjoram

2½ pounds venison steaks

2 tablespoons olive oil

2 handfuls hickory chips, soaked in water for 1 hour

 In a large, non-reactive bowl, stir together the stout, salt, honey, onions, Worcestershire

sauce, garlic, Tabasco sauce, bay leaves, pepper, chili powder, and marjoram. Add the steaks and completely submerge in the brine. Cover and refrigerate for 72 hours, turning the steaks twice daily. Drain and discard the brine. Lightly rinse the steaks and pat dry. Rub on all sides with the olive oil.

Prepare a low charcoal fire. Arrange coals in a ring around the perimeter of the grill. Drain the hickory chips and sprinkle half of the hickory chips over the fire. Place the steaks in the center of the rack. Cover the grill and smoke for 1 hour. Sprinkle the remaining hickory chips over the fire and add additional charcoal briquettes if necessary. Continue to smoke 1 to 2 additional hours, depending on the thickness of the meat.

Serves 6

Serve with Anderson Valley Brewing Company Poleeko Gold Pale Ale

Bear Republic Brewing Company

Founded by father-son team Richard and Richard Norgrove with the active assistance of their entire family, Bear Republic has skyrocketed to the top of America's must-visit microbreweries. Richard Jr. began his career as the production manager for a custom bicycle manufacturer where his homebrew first gained acclaim as "the best new product" at Interbike, the largest international bicycle trade show. After a stint at another brewery, he and his father spent two years researching microbreweries before deciding to locate their family-friendly brewpub in Healdsburg in the heart of Sonoma's wine country. Do yourself a favor and visit this excellent and friendly brewery the next time you are in Northern California.

Santa Fe Chicken Salad

Try this most satisfying main course salad on a hot summer night.

Grilled Chicken:

1/2 cup olive oil

1/4 cup chopped garlic

2 tablespoons minced fresh cilantro

1 teaspoon salt

1/2 teaspoon freshly ground black pepper

8 skinless boneless chicken breasts

Chile Vinaigrette:

1 1/2 cups olive oil

1/4 cup chopped cilantro

1/4 cup diced roasted red bell peppers

1/4 cup diced roasted Anaheim chiles

1/4 cup balsamic vinegar

1/4 cup red wine vinegar

1/4 cup white wine vinegar

2 tablespoons sugar

1 teaspoon minced garlic

1 teaspoon freshly squeezed lime juice

1 teaspoon Tabasco sauce

(continued on next page)

29

1 teaspoon chili powder

1 teaspoon cumin

1 teaspoon oregano

1/2 teaspoon salt

1/4 teaspoon freshly ground black pepper

2 cups roasted red bell peppers, julienned

2 cups diced tomatoes

2 avocados, diced

1 small red onion, thinly sliced

6 cups chopped Romaine hearts

1 cup pine nuts, lightly toasted

For the chicken: In a shallow dish, whisk together the olive oil, garlic, cilantro, salt, and pepper. Add the chicken breasts and turn to coat. Cover and chill in the refrigerator for 1 hour.

Prepare a hot grill. Remove the chicken from the marinade and discard the marinade. Grill chicken breasts on both sides until cooked through. When cool enough to handle, cut into 1/2-inch cubes. Set aside.

For the vinaigrette: In a large bowl, whisk together the olive oil, cilantro, diced red bell pepper, Anaheim chiles, balsamic vinegar, red wine vinegar, white wine vinegar, sugar, garlic, lime juice, Tabasco sauce, chili powder, cumin, oregano, salt, and pepper. Add the reserved chicken and toss to coat. Add the julienned red bell peppers, tomatoes, avocados, and red onion and toss to coat.

Divide the chopped lettuce onto 8 large plates. Arrange the chicken mixture evenly on top of the lettuce. Sprinkle with pine nuts and serve immediately.

Serves 8

Serve with Bear Republic Brewing Company Red Rocket Ale

Roasted Elephant Garlic

Sandy Poze, Bear Republic's in-house chef, has come up with the best roasted garlic I have ever tasted. With the baguette and the Brie, this makes an easy appetizer, a great snack, or even a light lunch on a cold day.

4 heads elephant garlic

1 cup olive oil

1 cup dry white wine

1 tablespoon chopped parsley

1 teaspoon minced fresh rosemary

1 teaspoon kosher salt

$1/4$ teaspoon freshly ground black pepper

1 baguette, thinly sliced diagonally

$1/2$ cup melted butter

8 ounces Brie cheese, cut into 16 pieces

2 roasted red bell peppers, thinly sliced

1 Granny Smith apple, cored and thinly sliced

Preheat oven to 375 degrees F. Lightly oil a 9 by 9-inch baking dish.

Remove the papery outer skins from the garlic, leaving the whole heads intact. Slice $1/2$ inch off the top. Place the garlic, cut-side up, into the prepared baking dish. Pour the olive oil and wine over the garlic. Sprinkle evenly with parsley, rosemary, salt, and pepper. Cover tightly with foil and roast for about 50 minutes, or until garlic is very tender. Remove from the oven and cool slightly.

Arrange sliced baguette on a baking sheet and brush with melted butter. Bake for 10 to 15 minutes, or until slightly golden.

To serve, place warm roasted garlic on a large platter. Place the Brie and roasted red bell pepper strips around the garlic. Fan the baguette slices and apple slices around the edge of the platter.

Serves 8

 **Serve with Bear Republic Brewing Company Red Rocket Ale**

Drunken Clams

This recipe is equally good if you substitute fresh mussels for the clams!

1/4 cup olive oil

2 tablespoons chopped garlic

1/2 cup diced Roma tomatoes

1/4 cup chopped fresh basil

3 cups Bear Republic Brewing Company
   XP Pale Ale

1/2 cup chicken stock

1/4 cup dry white wine

2 tablespoons freshly squeezed lemon juice

1/2 teaspoon salt

1/4 teaspoon freshly ground black pepper

2 pounds Manila clams

In a large pot, heat the olive oil over medium heat. Add the garlic and sauté until fragrant. Stir in the tomatoes and basil and sauté for 3 minutes. Stir in the ale, chicken stock, wine, lemon juice, salt, and pepper. Increase heat to high and bring to a boil. Add the clams, cover, and steam for about 3 minutes until clams open. Transfer clams to a large serving bowl. Discard any that do not open. Pour broth over clams and serve.

Serves 4

Serve with Bear Republic Brewing Company XP Pale Ale

Split Pea and Ham Soup
WITH PALE ALE

Sandy Poze serves this heart-warming soup at the brewery with fresh sourdough bread.

2 tablespoons vegetable oil

1 cup diced onions

$1/2$ cup diced carrots

$1/2$ cup diced celery

1 cup Bear Republic Brewing Company XP Pale Ale

6 cups chicken stock

3 cups water

$1^1/4$ pounds green split peas

1 teaspoon salt

$1/2$ teaspoon freshly ground white pepper

$1/2$ teaspoon thyme

1 bay leaf

8 ounces finely diced ham

In a large pot, heat the vegetable oil over medium heat. Add the onions, carrots, and celery and sauté until tender. Stir in the ale and bring to a simmer. Stir in chicken stock, water, split peas, salt, white pepper, thyme, and bay leaf and bring to a simmer. Reduce heat to medium-low and simmer until split peas are very tender, stirring often. Stir in the ham and heat through.

Serves 10

Serve with Bear Republic Brewing Company XP Pale Ale

Black and Blue Burger

If you are bearish on flavor, then this blue-cheese accented burger is just for you.

Roasted Red Pepper Mayonnaise:

1 cup mayonnaise

2 tablespoons roasted red pepper purée

1 teaspoon Cajun blackening spice blend

3 pounds ground chuck

Cajun blackening spice blend

$1^{1}/_{2}$ cups crumbled blue cheese

8 onion rolls, sliced in half and toasted

16 slices bacon, cooked until crisp

2 avocados, sliced

8 slices red onion

8 tomato slices

8 lettuce leaves

For the red pepper mayonnaise: In a bowl, whisk together mayonnaise, red pepper purée, and 1 teaspoon Cajun blackening spice until smooth. Cover and chill in the refrigerator for 1 hour to allow flavors to marry.

Prepare a hot grill. Form the ground beef into eight 6-ounce patties. Coat liberally with Cajun blackening spice blend. Grill the burgers to desired doneness. Top each buger with 3 table-spoons blue cheese and melt under a broiler. Spread the onion rolls with red pepper mayon-naise. Place a burger on a roll and top with 2 slices of bacon and 4 slices of avocado. Add red onion, tomato, and lettuce and serve immediately.

Serves 8

Serve with Bear Republic Brewing Company Racer 5 India Pale Ale

Ploughman's Supper WITH ALE-INFUSED CARAMELIZED ONIONS

Many a winegrower in Sonoma slakes his thirst and appetite with the ploughman's supper and a pint of pale ale.

Ale-Infused Caramelized Onions:

1/4 cup butter

4 onions, sliced

2 cups Bear Republic Brewing Company Racer 5 India Pale Ale

1 cup dry white wine

1/4 cup sugar

1 1/2 teaspoons salt

1/2 teaspoon freshly ground black pepper

4 rectangles puff pastry, approximately 5 inches x 7 1/2 inches

4 slices Gruyère cheese

4 (6-ounce) smoked bratwurst sausages

Whole grain mustard as an accompaniment

 Preheat oven to 400 degrees F.

For the onions: In a large skillet, melt the butter

over medium-high heat. Add the onions and toss to coat. Stir in the ale, wine, sugar, salt, and pepper and bring to a simmer. Cook, stirring often, until most of the liquid has evaporated. Cover skillet and reduce heat to medium-low. Continue to cook, stirring often, until onions turn a deep golden brown and are very tender.

Place a rectangle of puff pastry on a clean, dry work surface. Place a piece of cheese on top of the pastry and sausage on top of the cheese. Moisten the edges of the puff pastry and pinch together to seal. Place on a baking sheet. Repeat with remaining ingredients. Bake for about 20 minutes, or until golden brown. Remove from the oven and top with the caramelized onions. Serve immediately with mustard on the side.

Serves 4

Serve with Bear Republic Brewing Company Racer 5 India Pale Ale

Grilled Salmon
WITH AVOCADO SALSA

This recipe is a great example of what California cuisine is all about.

Avocado Salsa:

2 avocados, cut into $1/2$-inch cubes

$1/4$ cup diced red bell pepper

$1/4$ cup diced red onion

$1/4$ cup diced tomato

3 tablespoons minced fresh cilantro

3 tablespoons minced scallions

3 tablespoons olive oil

2 tablespoons balsamic vinegar

1 tablespoon freshly squeezed lime juice

1 teaspoon freshly ground black pepper

1 teaspoon chili powder

1 teaspoon salt

1 teaspoon Tabasco sauce

$1/4$ teaspoon cumin

1$^{1}/_2$ pounds salmon fillet, cut into 4 pieces

1 cup Cajun blackening spice blend

2 cups shredded green cabbage

$^1/_4$ cup shredded red cabbage

4 sprigs cilantro, for garnish

For the salsa: In a bowl, gently stir together the avocados, bell pepper, onion, tomato, cilantro, scallions, olive oil, vinegar, lime juice, pepper, chili powder, salt, Tabasco sauce, and cumin. Cover and chill in the refrigerator for 30 minutes.

Prepare a hot grill. Coat the salmon on both sides with the blackening spice and let stand at room temperature for 15 minutes. Transfer the salmon to the grill and cook on both sides until the fish just flakes.

(continued on next page)

Combine the green cabbage and red cabbage together in a large bowl. Divide onto four plates. Place the salmon on top of the cabbage. Spoon the avocado salsa on top of the salmon and garnish with a sprig of cilantro.

Serves 4

Serve with Bear Republic Brewing Company Racer 5 India Pale Ale

Without question, the greatest invention in the history of mankind is beer. Oh, I grant you that the wheel was also a fine invention, but the wheel does not go nearly as well with pizza.

Dave Barry

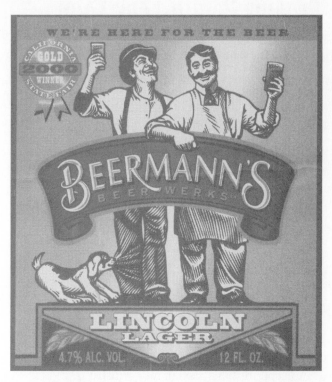

Beerman's Beerwerks and Meat Market

The combination of a great beer and a perfectly grilled steak is the beer lover's idea of 'died and gone to heaven.' Beerman's Beerwerks and Meat Market offers just such an otherworldly experience at their brewpub in California's Sierra foothills. Brewmaster Brian Ford is a master at creating the kind of brews that pair perfectly with both their casual pub fare as well as with their classic steakhouse menu. Award-winning beers are on tap at their hospitable pub just a short drive from Sacramento in the town of Lincoln.

Creamy Potato-Leek Soup
WITH CAVIAR

The intense flavor of black caviar elevates the
classic potato leek soup to the sublime.

4 slices uncooked bacon, minced

2 leeks, white and pale green part only, chopped

4 cups dry white wine

2 pounds red potatoes, peeled and diced

8 cups chicken stock

4 cups heavy cream

Salt and freshly ground black pepper, to taste

3 tablespoons black caviar, for garnish

 In a large pot, cook the bacon and leeks over medium heat until leeks are very tender. Stir in wine. Add the potatoes, chicken stock, cream, salt, and pepper. Reduce heat to medium-low and simmer until potatoes are very tender. In a blender or food processor, purée until very smooth. Heat through and ladle into bowls. Garnish each bowl with 1 teaspoon black caviar. Serve immediately.

Serves 10

 **Serve with Beerman's Beerwerks and Meat Market Lincoln Lager**

B J's Restaurant and Brewery

Under the direction of head brewer Alex Puchner, over thirty B J's restaurants are supplied with the freshest and finest of deluxe handcrafted beers. Located throughout Southern California, Colorado, Hawaii, Oregon, and Washington, Alex's beers find their way at B J's to happy and fun loving aficionados of their excellent cuisine. B J's is proof positive of the impact that handmade, premium crafted microbrews have had on America's cuisine.

Italian Chopped Salad

Hefeweizen is the epitome of a summer brew and what better accompaniment than this colorful summer salad.

1 head Romaine lettuce, finely chopped

$1/2$ cup diced marinated artichoke hearts

$1/2$ cup sliced black olives

$1/2$ cup diced red bell pepper

$1/2$ cup chopped scallions

$1/2$ cup freshly grated Parmesan cheese

$1/2$ cup diced salami

$1/3$ cup diced mozzarella cheese

$1/4$ cup canned garbanzo beans, drained

$1/2$ cup Italian salad dressing

$2/3$ cup diced tomatoes

In a large bowl, combine the lettuce, artichoke hearts, olives, bell pepper, scallions, Parmesan, salami, mozzarella, and garbanzo beans. Pour salad dressing over and toss well to coat. Sprinkle with tomatoes and serve immediately.

Serves 4 to 6

Serve with B J's Restaurant and Brewery Harvest Hefeweizen

Boston Beer Works

Beer and baseball. Can't go wrong. Toss in one of America's best ball-parks and finest breweries and you've got a home run. Across from Fenway Park, Boston Beer Works has been brewing up a series of hits since its opening in April of 1992. Consistently one of the top ten brewpubs in America, Boston Beer Works is one hell of a major-leaguer with a trophy case full of medals and tons of glowing reviews by local and national media for its great batting average. This ain't your daddy's baseball ballpark brew, and if your beerman doesn't bring you a mug of these suds, you gotta cry foul.

Bouden Balls
WITH SPICY TOMATO SAUCE

Boston Beer Works chef Bootsy Muller is no stranger to the dugout as these prove: he's got Bouden Balls.

Spicy Tomato Sauce:

2 tablespoons butter

1 onion, finely chopped

2 ribs celery, finely chopped

$1/2$ cup chopped green bell pepper

1 teaspoon chopped garlic

3 cups chopped tomatoes

$1/2$ teaspoon sugar

$1/2$ teaspoon Tabasco sauce

$1/2$ teaspoon Paul Prudholm Vegetable Magic Seasoning or other Cajun seasoning

Bouden Balls:

1 tablespoon olive oil

1 cup arborio rice

2 cups vegetable stock

4 ounces tasso or other smoked ham, minced

2 ounces fontina cheese, grated

(continued on next page)

1 cup all-purpose flour

1 tablespoon Paul Prudholm Vegetable Magic seasoning or other Cajun seasoning

3 eggs, beaten

2 tablespoons white wine Worcestershire sauce

2 cups panko bread crumbs

Oil for frying

1/2 cup freshly grated Parmesan cheese

3 scallions, chopped

For the tomato sauce: In a saucepan, melt the butter over medium heat. Add the onion, celery, bell pepper, and garlic and sauté until tender. Stir in tomatoes, sugar, Tabasco sauce, and Cajun seasoning and simmer, stirring often, until tomatoes are very tender. Remove from heat and set aside.

For the bouden balls: In a large saucepan, heat the olive oil over medium heat. Add the rice and toss to coat. In a separate saucepan, bring the vegetable stock to a simmer over medium-low heat. Ladle enough simmering stock into the rice to just cover the rice. Decrease the heat under the rice to medium-low and stir constantly until rice has almost absorbed all of the liquid. Add more simmering stock to just cover the rice and

continue stirring until almost absorbed. Repeat this process until the rice is tender but still firm. This will take about 20 minutes. Remove from heat and stir in the tasso and fontina. Spread mixture into a pie plate and let cool.

In a shallow bowl, sir together the flour and Cajun seasoning. In a separate shallow bowl, whisk together the eggs and Worcestershire sauce. Place the bread crumbs into a separate shallow bowl. Form about a tablespoon of the rice mixture into a ball. Roll in the flour mixture. Dip into the egg mixture and then coat with the bread crumbs. Place on a plate. Repeat until all the rice mixture is used.

In a large skillet, heat 1 inch of oil over medium-high heat. When the oil is hot, add the breaded balls and cook until well browned and crispy on all sides. Remove with a slotted spoon and drain on paper towels. Reheat the sauce and divide onto 6 plates. Place 3 bouden balls on top of the sauce and sprinkle with Parmesan and scallions. Serve immediately.

Serves 6

 **Serve with Boston Beer Works Bock Boy IPA**

Sugar-Seared Salmon

This recipe of Bootsy Muller's has more finesse than a double curve knuckleball. The flavors dance more than a shortstop with a runner leading off second. Enjoy when the salmon are running and the balls are flying!

1 (2-pound) salmon fillet, boneless and skinless

1 cup raw sugar

1/4 cup peanut oil

2 cups dry white wine

3 cups vegetable stock

1/4 cup butter

1 teaspoon salt

2 1/2 cups basmati rice

2/3 cup tamarind purée

Preheat oven to 400 degrees F.

Heat the peanut oil in a large cast iron skillet over medium-high heat. Coat salmon with the raw sugar. Place the salmon in the skillet and sear on one side. Turn salmon over and pour in the white wine. Place skillet in the oven and cook until fish just flakes, about 20 minutes.

In a saucepan, bring vegetable stock, butter, and salt to a boil over high heat. Stir in the basmati rice, reduce heat to medium-low, cover, and simmer for 20 minutes, or until all of the liquid is absorbed. Fluff rice and spoon onto a serving platter. Top with the salmon fillet. Drizzle tamarind purée over the salmon.

Serves 6

 Serve with Boston Beer Works Hay Market Hefeweizen

Grilled Flank Steak with Spicy Corn and Poblano Sauce AND Chorizo Mashed Potatoes

Bootsy Muller has a superb knack for creating new and delicious flavor combinations. Here's another winner!

Spicy Corn and Poblano Sauce:

1 cup corn kernels

1 cup beef stock

$1/2$ cup finely chopped poblano chile

$1/4$ cup prepared barbecue sauce

2 tablespoons butter

2 tablespoons minced roasted garlic

Salt and freshly ground black pepper, to taste

Chorizo Mashed Potatoes:

3 pounds Idaho potatoes, peeled and cut into quarters

1 cup heavy cream

4 ounces chorizo sausage, cooked and crumbled

2 tablespoons butter

2 tablespoons minced roasted garlic

Salt and freshly ground black pepper, to taste

2½ pounds flank steak, lightly scored on both sides

Salt and freshly ground black pepper, to taste

For the sauce: In a saucepan, combine the corn, beef stock, poblano, barbecue sauce, butter, garlic, salt, and pepper. Bring to a boil, then reduce heat to medium-low and simmer for 10 minutes. Remove from heat and keep warm.

For the potatoes: Bring a large pot of salted water to a boil. Add the potatoes and cook until tender. Drain potatoes in a colander. Return pot to the stove and add cream, chorizo, butter, roasted garlic, salt, and pepper and bring to a simmer over medium-low heat. Return the potatoes to the pot and mash together with the cream mixture. Remove from heat and keep warm.

(continued on next page)

Prepare a hot grill. Season flank steak with salt and pepper. Grill on both sides until done. Transfer steak to a cutting board and slice thinly across the grain. Divide mashed potatoes onto 6 plates. Top with several slices of flank steak and ladle sauce over the top.

Serves 6

 **Serve with Boston Beer Works Hay Market Hefeweizen**

Beer is proof that God loves us and wants us to be happy.

Benjamin Franklin

Deschutes
Brewery

Up in the land of Oregon where microbreweries practically outnumber inhabitants lies this brewery named after the clean-running Deschutes River. Located in the world-class ski town of Bend, the cold-conditioned ales are designed to quench the thirst of the most avid mogul hopper. The beer has flowed since 1988, and Deschutes is now one of the leading Northwest microbreweries. You can find their clean and refreshing suds at any number of premium restaurants throughout the Pacific Northwest.

Creamy Leek and Celeriac Soup

Celeriac, the bulbous root of a type of celery, has got to be tasted to be appreciated. Enjoy this creamy hot and hearty soup when the snow is still sticking to your powder pants.

2 tablespoons olive oil

3 pounds celeriac, peeled and diced

1 bunch leeks, white and pale green part only, sliced

1 tablespoon minced garlic

8 cups chicken stock

2 tablespoons lemon juice

1 bay leaf

2 cups heavy cream

Salt and freshly ground black pepper, to taste

1/2 cup snipped fresh chives, for garnish

In a large pot, heat the olive oil over medium heat. Add the celeriac and leeks and sauté until leeks are tender. Add the garlic and sauté until fragrant. Stir in the chicken stock, lemon juice, and bay leaf and bring to a simmer. Reduce heat to medium-low and simmer, stirring occasionally, until celeriac is very tender. Purée in a blender or food processor in batches, and return to pot. Stir in the cream, salt, and pepper and bring to a simmer. Continue to cook for about 15 minutes, or until slightly reduced. Divide into 8 bowls and sprinkle each with about 1 tablespoon chives.

Serves 8

Serve with Deschutes Brewery Bond Street Brown Ale

Penn Cove Mussels in Roasted Red Pepper Broth and Chipolata Sausage

OK, we said Penn Cove mussels, but we really mean any good fresh mussels. (What is important is that you have plenty of suds to enjoy. Keep your priorities straight and don't get caught up in the details.)

2 cups water

1 cup dry white wine

4 roasted red bell peppers, puréed

4 cloves garlic, minced

2 bay leaves

1 teaspoon thyme

6 whole peppercorns

Salt to taste

1 pound chipolata sausages, finely diced

2 pounds Penn Cove or your favorite mussels

In a large pot, combine the water, wine, red bell pepper purée, garlic, bay leaves, thyme, peppercorns, and salt. Bring to a boil over medium-high heat and simmer for 3 minutes. Stir in the sausages. Increase heat to high and bring to a boil. Add mussels, cover, and steam for about 3 minutes, or until mussels open. Transfer mussels to a large serving bowl. Discard any mussels that do not open. Pour broth over mussels and serve.

Serves 4

Serve with Deschutes Brewery Quail Springs IPA

Full Sail Brewing Company

The Columbia River Gorge is home to some of the finest windsurfing in the world, and the center of this windy paradise is Hood River where the world renowned Full Sail Ales are brewed. The first Oregon brewery to offer up its beers in bottles, the brewing is now divided between its original brewery in Hood River and a second Brew House/Pub in downtown Portland. This is easily one of the most popular beers in Oregon, and it takes only a couple of sips to see why.

Santa Fe
Pale Ale Salad

This salad features spicy black beans, savory grilled chicken breasts, and greens tossed with a cilantro-lime dressing on top of a warm tortilla.

Marinated Chicken:

1 cup Full Sail Brewing Company Pale Ale

2 tablespoons minced fresh cilantro

2 tablespoons freshly squeezed lime juice

4 cloves garlic, minced

Salt and freshly ground black pepper, to taste

4 boneless skinless chicken breasts

Black Beans:

2 tablespoons vegetable oil

1 onion, finely chopped

2 ancho chiles, finely diced

1 can (15 ounces) black beans

2 cups chopped tomatoes

1/4 cup Full Sail Brewing Company Pale Ale

1 teaspoon oregano

(continued on next page)

Cilantro-Lime Dressing:

$1/4$ cup chopped cilantro

$1/4$ cup freshly squeezed lime juice

2 shallots, chopped

1 tablespoon Dijon mustard

1 teaspoon chopped garlic

1 teaspoon sugar

$1/2$ teaspoon salt

$3/4$ cup vegetable oil

8 cups salad greens

4 Roma tomatoes, chopped

4 tortillas, warmed

For the chicken: In a shallow dish, whisk together the ale, cilantro, lime juice, garlic, salt, and pepper. Place the chicken breasts in the marinade, cover, and chill in the refrigerator for 1 hour, turning once.

Remove chicken from the marinade. Discard the marinade. Grill or broil until cooked through.

For the black beans: In a saucepan, heat the vegetable oil over medium heat. Add the onion and ancho chiles and sauté until tender. Stir in the black beans, tomatoes, ale, and oregano and bring to a simmer. Reduce heat to medium-low, partially cover saucepan, and simmer for 1 hour, stirring occasionally.

For the dressing: In the bowl of a food processor, combine cilantro, lime juice, shallots, Dijon mustard, garlic, sugar, and salt and process until smooth. With the motor running, add the vegetable oil in a thin stream until it is completely incorporated. Pour dressing into a large bowl. Add the salad greens and Roma tomatoes and toss to coat.

Divide warm tortillas onto 4 plates. Spread the black beans in the middle of each tortilla. Mound the salad greens on top of the black beans. Place the grilled chicken breasts on top of the greens. Serve immediately.

Serves 4

 **Serve with Full Sail Brewing Company Pale Ale**

Golden Pacific Brewing Company

There is hardly any other business where so many folks have started out in their garages and have progressed to their own boardroom. Golden Pacific was just such a success story. Started in 1981 by a home-brewer who hit on the right formula, and originally known as Thousand Oaks, it combined in 1990 with another small brewery and was renamed Golden Pacific Brewing Company. Originally set up to brew lagers, Golden Pacific, with its capacity of 40,000 barrels per year, has since branched out into ales. Located in Berkeley, California, Golden Pacific is in the right place to supply beer lovers of the greater Bay Area with premium hand-brewed beers.

Chinese Chicken Salad

Sandy Sachs assures me that a trip to the Asian market for the rice sticks is well worth the effort for this salad.

1 cup rice wine vinegar

1/2 cup honey

1/4 cup sesame oil

1 tablespoon salt

1 tablespoon freshly ground black pepper

1 teaspoon dry mustard

1 1/4 cups vegetable oil

4 cups cooked diced chicken breasts

4 cups finely chopped Romaine lettuce

1 cup bean sprouts

1 red bell pepper, julienned

1 yellow bell pepper, julienned

1/2 cup cashews, lightly toasted

1/2 cup snow peas, cut in half

(continued on next page)

Vegetable oil for frying

10 wonton skins, thinly sliced

2 ounces rice sticks, pulled apart into pieces

2 mangos, peeled and sliced, for garnish

2 avocados, peeled and sliced, for garnish

In a large bowl, whisk together the rice wine vinegar, honey, sesame oil, salt, pepper, and dry mustard until salt dissolves. Whisk in the vegetable oil. Add the chicken, lettuce, bean sprouts, red bell pepper, yellow bell pepper, cashews, and snow peas and toss to coat. Set aside.

In a wok or skillet, heat $1/2$-inch vegetable oil over high heat. Add the wonton skins and quickly stir-fry until golden brown. Remove wontons with a slotted spoon and drain on paper towels. Add rice sticks to the wok and as soon as they puff up, turn with tongs and push back into the oil. When crispy, remove with a slotted spoon and drain on paper towels.

Divide salad onto 6 large plates. Top with fried wonton skins and fried rice sticks. Garnish with mangos and avocados. Serve immediately.

Serves 6

Serve with Golden Pacific Brewing Company Amber Ale

Why, if 'tis dancing you would be,
There's brisker pipes than poetry.
Say, for what were hop-yards meant,
Or why was Burton built on Trent?
Oh many a peer of England brews
Livelier liquor than the Muse,
And malt does more than Milton can
To justify God's ways to man.
Ale, man, ale's the stuff to drink
For fellows whom it hurts to think:
Look into the pewter pot
To see the world as the world's not.

A. E. Housman

Curried Roasted Butternut Squash Soup

In the San Francisco Bay Area, long and rainy winter nights drive folks inside to sample Sandy Sachs' famous squash soup.

1 butternut squash

3 tablespoons butter

3 cups chopped onions

1 tablespoon curry powder

$1/4$ teaspoon freshly grated nutmeg

6 cups chicken stock

3 tablespoons Golden Pacific Brewing Company Hefeweizen

1 tablespoon honey

1 cup heavy cream

Salt and freshly ground black pepper, to taste

Snipped fresh chives, for garnish

Preheat oven to 350 degrees F. Lightly oil baking sheet.

Cut the squash in half lengthwise and scoop out seeds. Place squash cut-side down on the prepared baking sheet. Bake for about 45 minutes, or until very tender. When cool enough to handle, scoop out 3 cups of squash and set aside.

In a large pot, melt the butter over medium heat. Add the onions and sauté until translucent. Add the curry powder and nutmeg and sauté until fragrant. Stir in the chicken stock, beer, and honey and bring to a simmer. Reduce heat to medium-low, cover, and simmer gently for 30 minutes. Purée the soup in batches in a blender or food processor and return to pot. Stir in the cream, salt, and pepper. Heat through but do not let the mixture boil. Serve sprinkled with fresh chives.

Serves 6 to 8

 **Serve with Golden Pacific Brewing Company Hefeweizen**

Great Divide
Brewing Company

With a motto of "Great Minds Drink Alike," Brian and Tara Dunn founded their brewery in 1993, with the goal of providing Denver beer lovers with the best beer they've ever tasted. A few short years later, and with countless awards piling up on their beer bar, they have definitely reached their goal. Who knows what the future will bring, and who cares when such great beer is at hand in the mile high city.

Mango-Mint Salsa

This salsa is fabulous served with tortilla chips or grilled fish.

2 cups diced mango

1 red bell pepper, diced

$1/2$ cup finely minced red onion

$1/3$ cup chopped mint

2 jalapeño chiles, seeded and minced

Juice from 1 lime

In a bowl, stir together the mango, pepper, onion, mint, jalapeños, and lime juice. Cover and chill in the refrigerator for at least 1 hour to allow flavors to marry.

Serves 4 to 6

Serve with Great Divide Brewing Company Arapahoe Amber Ale

Gorgonzola Ale Soup

Creamy soups and good beer are a natural match. Search out a good ripe Gorgonzola for the best flavor.

1 tablespoon butter

1 onion, diced

4 cups chicken stock

2 cups Great Divide Brewing Company Arapahoe Amber Ale

2 pounds red potatoes, peeled and diced

12 ounces Gorgonzola cheese, crumbled

2 teaspoons freshly ground white pepper

2 teaspoons salt

2 cups heavy cream

Minced fresh chives, for garnish

In a large pot, melt the butter over medium heat. Add the onions and sauté until translucent. Stir in the chicken stock and ale and bring to a simmer. Add the potatoes and bring to a simmer. Reduce heat to medium-low, cover, and simmer until the potatoes are very tender.

In a blender, purée the soup in batches and return to pot. Bring to a simmer over medium heat and whisk in the Gorgonzola, pepper, and salt until smooth. Stir in the cream and heat through. Divide the soup into 8 bowls and sprinkle with chives. Serve immediately.

Serves 8

Serve with Great Divide Brewing Company Arapahoe Amber Ale

Spinach, Feta, and Sun-Dried Tomato Pizza

This recipe makes enough for two whole-wheat pizzas.

Pizza Dough:

2 cups warm water

1 package active dry yeast

$1/3$ cup olive oil

2 tablespoons sugar

$1^1/2$ teaspoons salt

1 cup whole-wheat flour

4 to $4^1/2$ cups all-purpose flour

Pour the warm water into a large bowl. Sprinkle the yeast over the top and let it dissolve. Stir in olive oil, sugar, and salt. Stir in whole-wheat flour and 4 cups all-purpose flour into the yeast mixture and combine until you have a soft dough. Add more flour if dough is sticky. Turn out onto a lightly floured surface and knead a few times until dough is smooth, about 5 minutes. Place dough into a lightly oiled bowl and turn to coat. Cover and let rise until doubled in bulk, about 1 hour.

Garlic Olive Oil:

2/3 cup olive oil

4 cloves garlic, minced

1/2 teaspoon basil

1/2 teaspoon oregano

In a small saucepan, combine the olive oil, garlic, basil, and oregano. Simmer over medium-low heat until fragrant. Remove from heat and set aside.

Toppings:

2 tablespoons olive oil

8 ounces baby spinach

1 cup sun-dried tomatoes packed in oil, chopped

8 ounces feta cheese, crumbled

12 ounces mozzarella cheese, shredded

4 ounces Romano cheese, grated

2 teaspoons oregano

(continued on next page)

Preheat oven to 400 degrees F.

In a large skillet, heat the olive oil over medium heat. Add the spinach and sauté until wilted. Transfer spinach to a cutting board and chop coarsely.

To assemble the pizzas: Punch dough down and divide into 2 balls. Flatten each ball into a disc about 12 inches in diameter and place on pizza pans or baking sheets. Brush the pizza dough with the reserved garlic oil. Divide the wilted spinach on top of each pizza. Sprinkle each with sun-dried tomatoes, feta, mozzarella, Romano, and oregano. Bake for 25 to 30 minutes, or until the crust is golden brown and the toppings are hot and bubbly.

Serves 12

Serve with Great Divide Brewing Company Arapahoe Amber Ale

Harbor Public House

Every great brewery needs enthusiastic public houses to serve their beer, and Jim and Judy Evans have provided the perfect venue to quaff a Northwest Microbrew on Bainbridge Island just outside of Seattle. Sit on their large deck with a dewy glass of brew and watch the Seattle skyline from across Eagle Harbor—so close to the city yet so removed from the hustle and bustle. Located in the Amanda and Ambrose Grow house, built in 1881, and refurnished with loving care, the Harbor Public House is one of the stalwart supporters of craft brewing.

Roasted Corn
and Halibut Stew

I can't wait until fresh corn hits the market to enjoy this savory halibut stew. If you can't find halibut, then substitute any coarse flake fish.

4 ears corn with husks

1/2 cup butter

3 ribs celery, chopped

1 onion, chopped

2 tablespoons minced garlic

1 1/2 pounds halibut, cut into 1-inch cubes

8 cups heavy cream

1 tablespoon minced fresh dill

Salt and freshly ground black pepper, to taste

Prepare a hot charcoal fire. Pull back the corn husks without tearing them off. Remove and discard the silk. Replace the corn husks and tie with kitchen string to keep them intact. Place the corn on the grill and cook on all sides until the husks are charred all over, about 15 minutes. When cool enough to handle, cut the kernels from the corn and reserve.

In a large pot, melt the butter over medium heat. Add the celery, onion, and garlic and sauté until the vegetables are tender but not browned. Add the halibut and sauté until opaque. Stir in the reserved corn kernels, cream, dill, salt, and pepper. Bring to a simmer, reduce heat to medium-low, and simmer gently for 5 minutes. Serve immediately.

Serves 8

 **Serve with Harbor Public House Amber Ale**

Crab Cakes with Lime Chow-Chow

For the very best crab cakes, try to find fresh Dungeness crab, the Northwest's own favorite.

Lime Chow-Chow:

1 cup sugar

1 cup distilled white vinegar

1/4 cup freshly squeezed lime juice

2 teaspoons mustard seed

1 teaspoon celery seed

1 teaspoon dry mustard

1/2 teaspoon turmeric

1 cup finely diced red bell pepper

1/2 cup finely diced onions

1 1/2 tablespoons cornstarch

2 tablespoons cold water

Crab Cakes:

1/2 cup minced onions

1/4 cup minced celery

1/4 cup mayonnaise

2 eggs

1 teaspoon Dijon mustard

1 teaspoon thyme

1 teaspoon Worcestershire sauce

1/2 teaspoon Tabasco sauce

1/4 teaspoon cayenne

1 pound crabmeat, picked over

8 ounces finely ground saltine crackers, divided

3 tablespoons butter

3 tablespoons vegetable oil

For the chow-chow: In a saucepan, combine the sugar, vinegar, lime juice, mustard seed, celery seed, dry mustard, and turmeric. Bring to a boil over medium-high heat and cook, whisking constantly, until the sugar dissolves. Reduce heat to medium-low and add the bell pepper and onions. Cook, stirring, for about 3 minutes, or until barely tender. In a small bowl, whisk together the cornstarch and cold water until smooth. Pour into the saucepan, whisking

(continued on next page)

85

constantly, until mixture is slightly thickened. Remove from heat and set aside.

For the crab cakes: In a large bowl, stir together the onions, celery, mayonnaise, eggs, Dijon mustard, thyme, Worcestershire sauce, Tabasco sauce, and cayenne until blended. Add the crabmeat and toss to combine. Add 1 cup of the ground saltine crackers and toss to combine. Place remaining ground saltine crackers in a shallow dish and set aside. Form the crab mixture into 12 patties. Coat each patty with remaining saltine crumbs. Place on a tray, cover with plastic wrap, and chill in refrigerator for at least 30 minutes.

In a large skillet, heat butter and oil over medium-high heat. Add the crab cakes and cook until nicely browned on both sides. Spoon some of the lime chow-chow onto 6 plates and top with 2 crab cakes per person.

Serves 6

 **Serve with Harbor Public House Amber Ale**

Poached Halibut Cheeks with Cous Cous and Blackberry Vinaigrette

Some of the advantages of living on the coast are the excellent fish markets where halibut cheeks are a seasonal delight. Combine them with Northwest blackberries for the vinaigrette and you have a phenomenal dinner to serve and enjoy.

Blackberry Vinaigrette:

1 cup blackberries, puréed and strained

1/4 cup freshly squeezed lime juice

1/4 cup sugar

1/4 cup red wine vinegar

1 teaspoon salt

1/8 teaspoon white pepper

2/3 cup vegetable oil

Poached Halibut Cheeks:

8 cups water

1 onion, sliced

1 rib celery, sliced

(continued on next page)

87

1 clove garlic, chopped

1 pound halibut cheeks, cut into 2-ounce portions

Cous Cous:

2 cups vegetable stock

Salt and freshly ground black pepper, to taste

I cup cous cous

1/4 cup toasted hazelnuts, chopped

Blackberries, for garnish

For the vinaigrette: In a bowl, whisk together the blackberry purée, lime juice, sugar, vinegar, salt, and pepper until smooth. Whisk in the oil until smooth. Set aside.

For the cous cous: In a saucepan, combine the vegetable stock, salt, and pepper and bring to a boil. Whisk in the cous cous, cover the saucepan, and remove from heat. Let stand for 10 minutes. Stir in the hazelnuts.

For the halibut: In a straight-sided skillet, combine the water, onion, celery, and garlic. Bring to a boil over medium heat and simmer for 5 minutes. Add the halibut cheeks and simmer until cooked through.

Divide cous cous onto 4 plates. Top with 2 portions each of halibut cheeks. Drizzle with blackberry vinaigrette and garnish with the whole blackberries.

Serves 4

 **Serve with Harbor Public House India Pale Ale**

Hermit hoar, in solemn cell,
Wearing out life's evening gray;
Smite thy bosom, sage, and tell,
What is bliss, and which the way?
Thus I spoke; and speaking sigh'd;
Scarce repressed a starting tear;—
When the smiling sage reply'd –
"Come, my lad, and drink some beer."

Samuel Johnson

Grilled Spicy Salmon
WITH BLACK BEAN SALSA

Black Bean Salsa:

2 cups cooked black beans

2 cups roasted corn kernels

1/2 cup minced onion

1/4 cup minced cilantro

1 jalapeño chile, minced

2 tablespoons minced garlic

2 tablespoons freshly squeezed lime juice

1 tablespoon cumin

1 tablespoon olive oil

1 teaspoon chili powder

1 teaspoon salt

1/4 teaspoon cayenne pepper

Marinade:

1 cup olive oil

1/2 cup minced cilantro

1/4 cup freshly squeezed lemon juice

1/4 cup minced onion

2 tablespoons minced garlic

2 tablespoons freshly squeezed lime juice

2 pounds salmon fillet

 **For the salsa:** In a bowl, stir together the black beans, corn, onions, cilantro, jalapeño, garlic, lime juice, cumin, olive oil, chili powder, salt, and cayenne. Cover and chill in the refrigerator overnight.

For the marinade: In a shallow dish, whisk together the olive oil, cilantro, lemon juice, onions, garlic, and lime juice. Place the salmon in the marinade, cover, and chill overnight in the refrigerator, turning the salmon once.

Prepare a hot grill. Remove the salmon from the marinade and pat dry. Discard the marinade. Transfer the salmon to the grill and cook until the fish just flakes. Serve topped with a dollop of the black bean salsa.

Serves 4

Serve with Harbor Public House India Pale Ale

Iron Hill Brewery and Restaurant

After spending a day digging mash out of the tuns, you need hearty food. The folks at Iron Hill know this and guarantee a happy full stomach to brewers and beer-lovers alike. Distinctive, full-flavored, hand-crafted beers stream from this brewery, and their restaurant delivers inspired, yet informal, regional cuisine. Their main objective has, and always will be, to produce food and beer that is affordable, tasty, and well crafted. Their staff is knowledgeable and courteous. They take pride in their comfortable, casual, worry- and hurry-free dining. That is the key to their success.

California Baby Spinach Salad with Sun-Dried Cherry and Wheat Beer Vinaigrette

Chef Dan Bethard is a master at combining seasonal ingredients for delightful dishes, and this unusual combination is a perfect example.

Marinated Mushrooms:

1/4 cup olive oil

1 pound cremini mushrooms

4 cloves garlic, minced

1 tablespoon minced fresh basil

1 tablespoon minced fresh parsley

1 tablespoon minced fresh rosemary

2 tablespoons sherry vinegar

Salt and freshly ground black pepper, to taste

Sun-Dried Cherry and Wheat Beer Vinaigrette:

1 cup sun-dried cherries

3/4 cup Iron Hill Brewery Raspberry Wheat Beer

1/2 cup apple juice

(continued on next page)

 **93**

1 shallot, chopped

2 teaspoons Dijon mustard

2 teaspoons sugar

$1/2$ cup olive oil

$1/4$ cup sherry vinegar

1 tablespoon red wine vinegar

Salt and freshly ground black pepper, to taste

1 pound baby spinach

1 cup crumbled feta cheese

2 roasted red bell peppers, thinly sliced

8 slices bacon, cooked until crisp then crumbled

For the mushrooms: In a skillet, heat the olive oil over medium heat. Add the mushrooms and sauté until tender. Add the garlic and sauté until fragrant. Stir in the basil, parsley, and rosemary and sauté 1 minute more. Remove from heat and stir in the sherry vinegar. Season with salt and pepper and set aside to cool.

For the vinaigrette: In a bowl, combine the cherries, beer, and apple juice and let stand 30 minutes. In the bowl of a food processor, combine the cherry mixture with the shallots, mustard, and sugar and process until smooth. With the motor running, pour in the olive oil in a thin stream. Add the sherry vinegar, red wine vinegar, salt, and pepper and pulse until blended. Transfer dressing to a large bowl.

Add the spinach to the dressing and toss until well coated. Divide the spinach onto 6 plates. Top with the reserved marinated mushrooms, feta cheese, red bell peppers, and bacon and serve immediately.

Serves 6

 **Serve with Iron Hill Brewery Raspberry Wheat Beer**

Iron Hill Clams
WITH FENNEL BEER BROTH

The slight licorice flavor from the Pernod is an excellent counterpoint to the full bodied flavors of the Anvil Ale.

1/4 cup olive oil

1 bulb fennel, chopped

4 cloves garlic, minced

2 cups chicken stock

1 cup Iron Hill Brewing Company Anvil Ale

1/2 cup clam juice

2 tomatoes, diced

2 tablespoons minced fresh parsley

1 tablespoon minced fresh basil

1 tablespoon Pernod, or other anise flavored liquor

1 1/2 teaspoons minced fresh rosemary

1 teaspoon sugar

Salt and freshly ground black pepper, to taste

50 to 60 littleneck clams

In a large pot, heat the olive oil over medium heat. Add the fennel and sauté until tender. Add the garlic and sauté until fragrant. Stir in chicken stock, ale, clam juice, tomatoes, parsley, basil, Pernod, rosemary, sugar, salt, and pepper. Increase heat to high and bring to a boil. Add the clams, cover, and steam for about 3 minutes until clams open. Transfer the clams to a large serving bowl. Discard any that do not open. Pour broth over the clams and serve immediately.

Serves 4 to 6

 **Serve with Iron Hill Brewery Anvil Ale**

Beerubaisse

Dan Bethard, chef at Iron Hill, took the Marseille favorite and recreated it into his own scrumptious signature dish. Amazing what one dangerous man with a skillet can accomplish.

1/4 cup olive oil

1 onion, thinly sliced

1 bulb fennel, thinly sliced

1 carrot, thinly sliced

1 1/2 cups Iron Hill Brewery Anvil Ale

8 cups clam juice

3 tomatoes, chopped

1 tablespoon tomato paste

2 bay leaves

1/4 teaspoon saffron threads

Salt and freshly ground black pepper, to taste

48 mussels, scrubbed and debearded

24 littleneck clams

24 large scallops

18 jumbo shrimp, shelled

1 pound cod fillet, cut into 6 pieces

2 tablespoons minced parsley

 In a large pot, heat the olive oil over medium heat. Add the onion, fennel, and carrot and sauté until tender. Pour in the ale and simmer until the liquid is reduced by half. Add the clam juice, tomatoes, tomato paste, bay leaves, saffron, salt, and pepper and bring to a boil. Reduce heat to medium and simmer for 30 minutes.

Add the mussels, clams, scallops, shrimp, and cod and simmer until the mussels and clams have opened and the cod is fully cooked. Discard any unopened mussels or clams. Stir in the chopped parsley. Divide the seafood into 6 bowls and ladle the broth on top. Serve immediately.

Serves 6

Serve with Iron Hill Brewery Anvil Ale

Bockwurst Sandwich
WITH APPLE AND ONION COMPOTE

We owe our appreciation of good wurst to the Germans, and Chef Dan Bethard has definitely improved on the standard sausage plate with this creation.

Apple and Onion Compote:

3 tablespoons olive oil

2 Granny Smith apples, peeled, cored, and diced

1 red onion, diced

2 tablespoons sherry vinegar

1 tablespoon honey

Salt and freshly ground black pepper, to taste

4 bockwurst sausages, butterflied

6 ounces ($^3/_4$ cup) Havarti cheese, shredded

1 bunch watercress

4 French rolls

For the compote: In a saucepan, heat the olive oil over medium heat. Add the apples and onions and sauté until golden and very tender. Add the vinegar, honey, salt, and pepper and simmer, stirring often, until almost all of the liquid has evaporated.

Preheat the broiler.

In an oven-proof skillet, brown the sausages on both sides. Top each sausage with the compote and cheese. Place under the broiler until the cheese is melted. Split the rolls and divide the watercress among them. Place a sausage into each roll and serve immediately.

Serves 4

 **Serve with Iron Hill Brewery Raspberry Wheat Beer**

Lejon Pizza

What can be more American than pizza and beer? Try Iron Hill's tasty variation on this standard favorite. You won't be disappointed.

Pizza Sauce:

1 cup mayonnaise

1/2 cup sour cream

1 1/2 tablespoons minced fresh chives

1 tablespoon horseradish

1 teaspoon freshly squeezed lemon juice

1/2 teaspoon Worcestershire sauce

Salt and freshly ground black pepper, to taste

1 24-inch unbaked pizza shell

6 slices uncooked bacon, chopped

8 ounces rock shrimp

3 scallions, sliced

1 1/2 cups shredded mozzarella cheese

2 teaspoons minced fresh parsley

Preheat oven to 350 degrees F.

For the sauce: In a bowl, whisk together the mayonnaise, sour cream, chives, horseradish, lemon juice, Worcestershire sauce, salt, and pepper until smooth. Place the pizza shell on baking sheet. Spread the sauce over pizza and set aside.

In a skillet, sauté the bacon over medium heat until crisp. Remove the bacon with a slotted spoon and sprinkle over pizza. Add the rock shrimp to the skillet and sauté until cooked through. Remove the shrimp with a slotted spoon and sprinkle over the bacon. Sprinkle with the scallions and top with the mozzarella. Bake for about 20 minutes, or until the crust is golden brown and the cheese is bubbly. Sprinkle with parsley and serve immediately.

Serves 8

 Serve with Iron Hill Brewery Anvil Ale

Sirloin Steak
WITH ALE-BRAISED MUSHROOMS AND CARAMELIZED ONIONS

Rosemary mashed potatoes would be a great side dish to sop up the extra sauce.

1/4 cup olive oil

1 Vidalia onion, chopped

1 pound cremini mushrooms, sliced

6 cloves garlic, minced

1 1/2 cups Iron Hill Brewery Anvil Ale

1/2 cup dry sherry

1/2 cup beef stock

2 tablespoons freshly squeezed lemon juice

1 tablespoon sherry vinegar

1/2 teaspoon sugar

Salt and freshly ground black pepper, to taste

2 tablespoons cornstarch

1/4 cup cold water

6 (12 ounces each) sirloin steaks

In a large skillet, heat the olive oil over medium heat. Add the onions and sauté until golden brown. Add the mushrooms and sauté until tender. Add the garlic and sauté until fragrant. Stir in the ale and dry sherry and bring to a simmer. Stir in the beef stock, lemon juice, sherry vinegar, sugar, salt, and pepper and bring to a simmer. In a small bowl, dissolve the cornstarch in cold water. Pour into the mushroom mixture and stir until slightly thickened. Remove from heat and keep warm.

Prepare a hot grill. Season the steaks with salt and pepper and grill to desired doneness. Place steaks on plates and divide the sauce over the steaks.

Serves 6

 **Serve with Iron Hill Brewery Anvil Ale**

Lost Coast Brewery

The story of the Lost Coast Brewery is the story of two fun-loving young ladies who followed their dream of having their own brewery. Instead of taking a normal career path, they journeyed to visit scores of pubs in England and Wales, jumped in with all four feet, and opened the Lost Coast Brewery and Café in 1986. Eureka, California, hasn't been the same since. They cajoled the local Knights of Pythias to sell them their 100-year old building, installed a brewpub and café, and have been selling great food and brewing fine beers in the Humboldt Bay region ever since.

Stout Beef Stew

When the fog rolls in and the chill settles over the land, thoughts turn to this hearty stew.

1^1/$_2$ cups all-purpose flour

1 tablespoon salt

2 teaspoons oregano

2 teaspoons freshly ground black pepper

2 teaspoons paprika

2 teaspoons thyme

1 teaspoon sage

3 pounds beef stew meat

^{1}/$_2$ cup vegetable oil

2 onions, chopped

1 stalk celery, chopped

5 cloves garlic, chopped

2 ^{3}/$_4$ cups Lost Coast Brewery 8-Ball Stout

1^1/$_2$ cups Lost Coast Brewery Downtown Brown Ale

1^1/$_2$ cups water

5 carrots, sliced

5 red potatoes, cut into ^{1}/$_2$-inch cubes

1 cup sour cream

(continued on next page)

Preheat oven to 350 degrees F.

In a shallow dish, combine the flour, salt, oregano, pepper, paprika, thyme, and sage and stir together with a fork until blended. In a large pot, heat the oil over medium-high heat. Dredge the meat in the flour mixture, shaking off the excess. Add to the pot and brown well on all sides. Add the onions, celery, and garlic and sauté until tender. Add the stout and ale and bring to a simmer. Stir in the water and bring to a simmer. Cover the pot and place in the oven. Bake for 1 hour. Add the carrots and potatoes, cover, and bake an additional 1 hour, or until the meat is very tender. Garnish each serving with a dollop of sour cream.

Serves 6

 Serve with Lost Coast Brewery 8-Ball Stout

Spicy Prawns

Although not off the Richter scale in terms of heat, these spicy prawns definitely do have a bit of back burn. Allow ample quantities of cold suds to slake the fire.

Seasoning Mix:

1 teaspoon freshly ground black pepper

1 teaspoon paprika

1/2 teaspoon dried red chile flakes

1/2 teaspoon rosemary, crumbled

1/2 teaspoon thyme

1/4 teaspoon oregano

48 large prawns with heads and shells

1 tablespoon olive oil

1 tablespoon minced garlic

6 tablespoons butter, divided

1 1/2 cups Lost Coast Brewery Downtown Brown Ale

French bread

(continued on next page)

For the seasoning mix: In a shallow dish, stir together the pepper, paprika, chile flakes, rosemary, thyme, and oregano with a fork.

Dredge the prawns in the seasoning mix, reserving any additional seasoning mix. In a large skillet, heat the olive oil over medium-high heat. Add the prawns and sauté for 1 minute. Add the garlic and sauté until fragrant. Add 3 tablespoons of the butter and any remaining seasoning mix and sauté until butter has melted. Stir in the ale and simmer for 2 minutes. Stir in the remaining butter until melted. Divide into 6 bowls and serve immediately with fresh crusty French bread.

Serves 6

Serve with Lost Coast Brewery Downtown Brown Ale

McGuire's Pub

With a tip of our bowler we have to salute one of America's premier tippling establishments. McGuire's Irish Pub in Pensacola, Florida, has over 20,000 square feet of pub space where stuffed moose heads and more than 150,000 dollar bills are pasted to the ceiling and walls. In 1988, McGuire's added a microbrewery, Florida's first, to their restaurant, and they now brew a complete range of ales, porters, and stouts as well as a genuine root beer, all made from the purest natural ingredients. McGuire's is the Holy Grail to everyone desiring a wee bit of the luck o' the Irish. When you are in Florida, make it a point to come kiss the Blarney stone, knock back a pint, and savor the food that the Irish are known for.

Three Cabbage Slaw

This delicious and pretty cole slaw is easy to make and the recipe can be doubled or tripled to serve a crowd.

1/4 cup apple cider vinegar

2 tablespoons brown sugar

1/2 teaspoon salt

1/4 teaspoon freshly ground black pepper

8 ounces (about 1 1/2 cups) green cabbage, coarsely shredded

8 ounces (about 1 1/2 cups) red cabbage, coarsely shredded

8 ounces (about 1 1/2 cups) Savoy cabbage, coarsely shredded

1 small unpeeled red apple, julienned

 In a small saucepan, stir together the vinegar, brown sugar, salt, and pepper. Bring to a simmer over medium-low heat, whisking constantly, until sugar dissolves. Remove from heat and set aside.

In a large bowl, combine the cabbages and apples. Pour the vinegar mixture over and toss well. Cover and chill thoroughly in the refrigerator before serving to allow flavors to marry. Toss again right before serving.

Serves 4

Serve with McGuire's Irish Ale

Famous Irish Fried Onion Rings

There's a good reason these tender crispy onion rings are famous, and when you taste them, you'll know why. Baskets of them go like wildfire at McGuire's.

6 cups saltine crackers (about 120 crackers)

1 teaspoon garlic powder

1 teaspoon onion powder

$1/2$ teaspoon paprika

$1/2$ teaspoon freshly ground black pepper

$1^1/2$ cups McGuire's Irish Ale

1 egg

$1/2$ teaspoon salt

2 cups all-purpose flour

4 cups vegetable oil

3 large yellow onions, sliced into $1/2$-inch rings

In the bowl of a food processor, process the saltine crackers in batches until you have coarse crumbs. Transfer saltine crumbs to a large bowl. Stir in the garlic powder, onion powder, paprika, and pepper. Set aside.

In a separate bowl, whisk together the ale, egg, and salt until smooth. Slowly mix in the flour, stirring well, until the mixture resembles thick pancake batter.

In a large deep skillet, heat the oil to 375 degrees F. Working in batches, dip each onion ring into the batter, then the cracker mixture. Drop into the hot oil and cook, turning once, until golden brown, about 1 to 2 minutes. With a slotted spoon, transfer the onion rings to paper towels to drain before serving.

Serves 6 to 8

 **Serve with McGuire's Irish Ale**

Pickled Beer-Boiled Shrimp

This is one of those blessedly convenient party foods you can prepare a day ahead of the event.

3 cups McGuire's Irish Ale

2 tablespoons pickling spice

1 pound large shrimp, shelled and deveined with tails left on

1 tablespoon Dijon mustard

1 teaspoon prepared horseradish

1 teaspoon celery salt

1/4 teaspoon freshly ground black pepper

2 scallions, chopped

1/4 cup vegetable oil

In a large pot, combine the ale and pickling spice and bring to a boil over medium-high heat. Add the shrimp and cook until just pink, about 2 or 3 minutes. With a slotted spoon remove the shrimp and pickling spice and set aside. Reserve $1/2$ cup of the broth and pour into a bowl. To the broth in the bowl, whisk in the Dijon mustard, horseradish, celery salt, pepper, and scallions. Slowly pour in the oil in a thin stream, whisking constantly, until the mixture is emulsified. Fold in the reserved shrimp and pickling spice. Cover and refrigerate overnight. Serve cold or at room temperature.

Serves 8 to 10

Serve with McGuire's Irish Ale

Honey and Beer Oven-Braised Ribs

Marinate these sticky-delicious ribs a day ahead.

$1/2$ cup honey

$1/2$ cup McGuire's Stout

1 tablespoon freshly squeezed lemon juice

$1^1/2$ teaspoons salt

1 teaspoon chili powder

1 teaspoon sage

$3/4$ teaspoon dry mustard

2 racks pork spareribs

In a small saucepan, stir together the honey, stout, lemon juice, salt, chili powder, sage, and dry mustard. Simmer over medium-low heat for 5 minutes. Remove from heat and let cool.

Place the ribs, meaty-side down, in a large roasting pan. Brush the ribs with the marinade. Cover and refrigerate overnight, turning the ribs over and basting them with the marinade about halfway through.

Preheat oven to 350 degrees F.

Bake the ribs, turning and basting them with marinade every 20 minutes, until tender, about 1 to 1 1/2 hours.

Serves 4

 **Serve with McGuire's Stout**

Sheep Dip

Serve this savory spread with French bread, crackers, or crisp breads.

1^1/$_3$ cups crumbled feta cheese

1 cup whole-milk ricotta cheese

2 tablespoons brandy

^{1}/$_4$ cup minced scallions

^{1}/$_4$ cup pine nuts, lightly toasted

3 tablespoons minced fresh dill

 In the bowl of a food processor or a blender, combine feta and ricotta and process until smooth. Add the brandy and process until blended. Transfer cheese-brandy mixture to a large bowl. Fold in the scallions, pine nuts, and dill until well blended. Spoon into a 2-cup crock or serving bowl. Cover and chill in the refrigerator for at least two hours to allow flavors to marry.

Serves 10

Serve with McGuire's Irish Ale

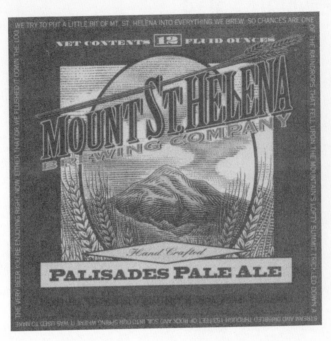

Mount St. Helena Brewing Company

A few miles north of the Napa Valley in Middletown, California, Mount St. Helena Brewing Company serves up tasty grub and cool suds to the wine-weary travelers. On the route to Interstate 5, the brewpub grills juicy steaks, bakes savory pizzas, and fills pitchers with their crystal clear cold beer for locals and travelers alike. Next trip to the wine country, make sure you pull off at the halfway point for a pint of some of the best beer around.

Potato Salad

Easily one of the tastiest potato salads I have ever encountered. It has since become my summer standard.

$1/4$ cup cider vinegar

1 tablespoon mustard seeds

2 cups mayonnaise

3 teaspoons salt

2 teaspoons sugar

$1/2$ teaspoon freshly ground black pepper

2 cups thinly sliced celery

1 cup finely chopped onions

1 cup sliced black olives

$2^1/2$ pounds red potatoes

In a large bowl, combine the vinegar and mustard seeds and let stand for 30 minutes. Whisk in the mayonnaise, salt, sugar, and pepper until smooth. Add celery, onions, and olives and toss to coat.

Boil the potatoes in their jackets until just tender. When cool enough to handle, peel the potatoes and cut into 1/2-inch cubes. Toss the warm potatoes with the dressing. Cover, and chill in the refrigerator for at least 3 hours to allow flavors to marry.

Serves 10

Serve with Mount St. Helena Brewing Company Palisades Pale Ale

Cheddar and Potato Soup

It takes rib-sticking food to get a farmer through a 12-hour day in the vineyards, and the success of Mount St. Helena's brewpub is due in no small measure to its kitchen.

2 cups water

2 cups peeled and diced potatoes

1/2 cup cooked and crumbled bacon

1/2 cup diced carrots

1/2 cup diced celery

1/4 cup finely chopped onions

1 teaspoon salt

1/4 teaspoon freshly ground black pepper

1/4 cup butter

1/4 cup all-purpose flour

2 cups milk

2 cups grated cheddar cheese

In a pot, combine the water, potatoes, bacon, carrots, celery, onions, salt, and pepper. Bring to a boil over medium heat, partially cover the pot, and simmer until the potatoes are very tender.

In a saucepan, melt the butter over medium heat. Whisk in the flour until smooth. Slowly whisk in the milk until it is completely incorporated. Simmer, whisking constantly, until slightly thickened. Remove from heat and stir in the cheddar cheese until smooth. Stir the cheese mixture into the potato mixture and heat through.

Serves 6

Serve with Mount St. Helena Brewing Company Palisades Pale Ale

Country Mushroom Soup

Fresh wild mushrooms definitely kick this soup up a notch, but if they're unavailable where you live, regular mushrooms will be delicious.

$1/3$ cup olive oil

$1^1/2$ cups chopped celery

$1/2$ cup chopped onions

2 pounds mushrooms, sliced

$1/2$ cup butter

$1/2$ cup all-purpose flour

4 cups chicken stock

2 bay leaves

1 teaspoon salt

$1/2$ teaspoon freshly ground black pepper

$1^1/3$ cups half-and-half

In a large skillet, heat the olive oil over medium heat. Add the celery and onions and sauté until tender. Add the mushrooms and sauté until tender and most of the liquid has evaporated. Set aside.

In a large pot, melt the butter over medium heat. Whisk in the flour until smooth and bubbly. Gradually whisk in the chicken stock until smooth. Add the bay leaves, salt, and pepper. Bring to a simmer, whisking constantly, until slightly thickened. Stir in the reserved mushroom mixture and bring to a boil. Reduce heat to medium-low and simmer, uncovered, for 15 minutes. Stir in the half-and-half and heat through.

Serves 6 to 8

Serve with Mount St. Helena Brewing Company Palisades Pale Ale

Mushroom and Spinach Lasagna

Mushroom and Spinach Filling:

1/4 cup olive oil

1 onion, chopped

1 green bell pepper, chopped

2 cloves garlic, minced

1 pound mushrooms, sliced

1 pound fresh spinach, washed and coarsely
  chopped

1 can (28 ounces) diced tomatoes

1 can (6 ounces) tomato paste

1 1/4 teaspoons oregano

1 teaspoon salt

1 pound lasagna noodles

1 pound mozzarella cheese, shredded

1 cup shredded cheddar cheese

3 tablespoons freshly grated Parmesan cheese

Preheat oven to 375 degrees F. Lightly oil a 9 x 13-inch baking dish.

For the filling: In a large pot, heat the olive oil over medium heat. Add the onion, green bell pepper, and garlic and sauté until the onion is translucent. Add the mushrooms and sauté until tender. Add the spinach and sauté until wilted. Add the diced tomatoes, tomato paste, oregano, and salt and simmer until slightly thickened, about 15 minutes. Set aside.

Bring a large pot of salted water to a boil. Add the lasagna to the water and cook for about 8 minutes. Do not overcook or the pasta will be difficult to handle. Drain well.

Layer half of the lasagna sheets in the bottom of the prepared baking dish, overlapping the pieces to cover the bottom completely. Spread half of the filling mixture evenly over the pasta.

(continued on next page)

Cover filling with half of the mozzarella and cheddar. Layer remaining pasta over the cheeses. Spread remaining filling over the pasta. Top with remaining mozzarella and cheddar cheese. Sprinkle Parmesan on top. Cover with foil and bake for 20 minutes. Remove the foil and continue baking for an additional 10 minutes, or until hot and bubbly.

Serves 6

 **Serve with Mount St. Helena Brewing Company Palisades Pale Ale**

Not all chemicals are bad.
Without chemicals such as hydrogen
and oxygen, for example,
there would be no way
to make water, a vital ingredient
in beer.

Dave Barry

California Salad
WITH POPPY SEED DRESSING

Walnuts and blue cheese are a classic combination. Try this variation with candied walnuts and Gorgonzola along with a pint of their pale ale.

Candied Walnuts:

1 cup sugar

$^1/_2$ cup water

2 cups walnuts

Poppy Seed Dressing:

$^1/_2$ cup sugar

$^1/_2$ cup olive oil

$^1/_2$ cup vegetable oil

$^1/_3$ cup cider vinegar

$^1/_4$ cup grated onion

1$^1/_2$ teaspoons poppy seeds

1 teaspoon dry mustard

1 teaspoon salt

(continued on next page)

 **131**

12 cups salad greens

2 apples, diced

1 cup crumbled Gorgonzola cheese

1 cup raisins

Preheat oven to 300 degrees F. Lightly oil a baking sheet.

For the walnuts: In a saucepan, stir together the sugar and water over medium heat until the sugar dissolves. Increase the heat to medium-high and stir in the walnuts. Cook, stirring often, until the mixture begins to caramelize and turn golden brown. Spread the walnuts onto the prepared baking sheet and bake for 20 to 25 minutes, or until they turn a deep golden brown. Place the baking sheet on a rack to cool. Break the walnuts into small pieces when cool enough handle.

For the dressing: In a bowl, whisk together the sugar, olive oil, vegetable oil, vinegar, onion, poppy seeds, dry mustard, and salt until smooth.

Toss the salad greens with the dressing and divide onto 6 plates. Top with the apples, Gorgonzola, raisins, and candied walnuts.

Serves 6

 **Serve with Mount St. Helena Brewing Company Palisades Pale Ale**

For a quart of Ale is a dish for a King.

William Shakespeare,
A Winter's Tale

Chicken Piccata

Similar to the schnitzels of Germany, this Italian version is guaranteed to please. Serve with rice pilaf.

4 boneless, skinless chicken breasts

All-purpose flour for dredging

2 tablespoons olive oil

1/4 cup dry white wine

2 tablespoons capers

2 tablespoons freshly squeezed lemon juice

1/2 teaspoon salt

1/4 teaspoon freshly ground black pepper

Place a piece of waxed paper over each chicken breast and pound the chicken breasts until they are $1/2$-inch thick. Dredge lightly in flour and shake off the excess. In a skillet, heat the olive oil over medium heat. Add the chicken and lightly brown on both sides. Add the wine, capers, lemon juice, salt, and pepper and bring to a simmer. Reduce heat to medium-low and continue to simmer until the chicken is cooked through and the sauce has slightly thickened. Transfer chicken to a platter and spoon the sauce on top.

Serves 4

Serve with Mount St. Helena Brewing Company Palisades Pale Ale

North Coast Brewing Company

Maybe it's the rainy winters or maybe it's the water that makes for great breweries, but either way one has to admit that Northern California and the Pacific Northwest have more than their share of outstanding beers. Since 1988, North Coast Brewing Company on California's Mendocino Coast has been doing its share to ensure a steady flow of the best brews to loyal beer lovers. Named "One of the 10 Best Breweries in the World" by the Beverage Testing Institute in Chicago, North Coast has, under the talented direction of Brewmaster Mark Ruedrich, established a reputation for exceptional quality and consistency. North Coast has also assumed a leadership role in the brewing industry in the artful pairing of food and beer.

Creole Shrimp

Serve this spicy dish over steamed rice.

Creole Spice Mixture:

$1/2$ teaspoon basil

$1/4$ teaspoon cayenne

$1/4$ teaspoon oregano

$1/4$ teaspoon paprika

$1/4$ teaspoon black pepper

$1/4$ teaspoon white pepper

$1/4$ teaspoon salt

$1/4$ teaspoon thyme

$1/3$ cup butter, divided

1 pound mushrooms, sliced

1 tablespoon minced garlic

1 tablespoon minced shallots

1 bay leaf

$1^1/2$ pounds large shelled shrimp

$1/4$ cup chicken stock

(continued on next page)

For the spice mixture: In a small bowl, stir together the basil, cayenne, oregano, paprika, black pepper, white pepper, salt, and thyme with a fork until blended. Set aside.

In a large skillet, melt 3 tablespoons of the butter over medium heat. Add the mushrooms, garlic, shallots, and bay leaf and sauté until the mushrooms are tender. Stir in the spice mixture. Add the shrimp and sauté until they just turn pink. Stir in the chicken stock and bring to a simmer. Stir in remaining butter and serve immediately.

Serves 4

Serve with North Coast Brewing Company Red Seal Ale

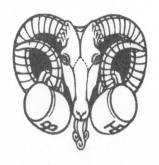

Chimayo Chicken Salad

The seasonings in this artful salad reflect the Hispanic heritage of California.

Dressing:

1/4 cup freshly squeezed lime juice

1 tablespoon red wine vinegar

2 cloves garlic, minced

2 teaspoons cumin

1 teaspoon Dijon mustard

3/4 teaspoon chili powder

1/2 teaspoon salt

1/4 teaspoon freshly ground black pepper

1/2 cup olive

2 cups diced grilled chicken

1 can (15 ounces) kidney beans, rinsed and drained

1 can (14 ounces) yellow hominy, rinsed and drained

6 cups mixed salad greens

1 avocado, peeled and thinly sliced

1 roasted red bell pepper, thinly sliced

12 cherry tomatoes, cut in half

1/4 cup chopped cilantro

(continued on next page)

For the dressing: In a bowl, whisk together the lime juice, vinegar, garlic, cumin, mustard, chili powder, salt, and pepper until smooth. Add the olive oil in a thin stream, whisking constantly, until all is incorporated. Add the chicken, kidney beans, and hominy and stir to coat. Cover and chill for 30 minutes to allow flavors to marry.

Divide salad greens onto 6 plates. Distribute the chicken mixture on top of the greens. Arrange the avocado, red pepper, and cherry tomatoes decoratively on top of the chicken mixture. Sprinkle with cilantro and serve immediately.

Serves 6

Serve with North Coast Brewing Company Scrimshaw Pilsner

Pennsylvania Brewing Company

It took a descendent of F. D. Pastorius, founder of the first German settlement in the United States, to recognize the potential locked up in the old Eberhardt and Ober Brewing Company. The old brewery, closed for more than ten years and located in the historic Deutschtown neighborhood of Philadelphia's North Side, was desperately in need of some tender loving care. Tom Pastorius was up to the challenge. Renamed the Pennsylvania Brewing Company, Tom and his German brewmaster have created over thirteen true lager-style beers. Tom's wife, Mary Beth and Chef Dan Dooley manage the restaurant, which is an authentic Bavarian-style "Gastwirtschaft." Long tables with bench-style seating encourage strangers to share conversation and get to know each other over a hearty meal and cool beer.

Wild Boar Pâté

If a wild boar doesn't happen to cross your path, you can substitute domestic pork with good results.

2 tablespoons butter

12 ounces (1^1/$_2$ cups) chicken breast, finely diced

12 ounces (1^1/$_2$ cups) boar meat, finely diced

6 ounces (^{3}/$_4$ cup) pork fatback, finely diced

2 cups minced onion

^{1}/$_2$ cup minced fresh parsley

2 tablespoons Madeira wine

2^1/$_2$ teaspoons salt

^{1}/$_2$ teaspoon freshly ground black pepper

^{1}/$_4$ teaspoon thyme

4 slices bacon

French bread

Cornichons

Preheat oven to 325 degrees F.

In a large skillet, melt the butter over medium heat. Add the diced chicken and sauté until lightly browned. Remove from heat and transfer chicken to a large bowl. Add the boar, pork fatback, onion, parsley, Madeira, salt, pepper, and thyme and stir together gently until well mixed. Pack mixture into a heavy terrine with a lid. Lay bacon slices over the top. Cover the terrine and place in a baking pan. Add enough water to baking pan to come halfway up the sides of the terrine. Bake for 1$^{1}/_{2}$ hours, or until internal temperature of the pâté reaches 140 degrees F on a meat thermometer. Remove from oven and set aside to cool. Chill in the refrigerator at least 8 hours or overnight before serving to allow flavors to marry. Cut into slices and serve with French bread and cornichons.

Serves 10

 **Serve with Pennsylvania Brewing Company Weizen**

Salmon Balls

Pop these savory nuggets of juicy salmon into your mouth and wash them down with a cold glass of Penn Gold Lager.

1 pound cooked salmon, flaked

2 cups peeled and grated potato

1 cup grated onion

1 egg

1 1/2 tablespoons all-purpose flour

1 teaspoon salt

1/2 teaspoon freshly ground black pepper

1 cup fine dry bread crumbs

Oil for frying

In a bowl, combine the salmon, potato, onion, egg, flour, salt, and pepper and mix well. Shape mixture into walnut-sized balls. Place bread crumbs in a shallow dish. Roll salmon balls in the bread crumbs, coating them completely. Arrange the salmon balls on a tray. Cover the salmon balls and chill in the refrigerator for at least 1 hour.

In a large skillet, heat 2 inches of oil to 350 degrees F. Place salmon balls in hot oil, a few at a time; do not crowd. Cook on all sides until golden brown. With a slotted spoon, transfer salmon balls to paper towels to drain. Serve hot.

Serves 4

Serve with Pennsylvania Brewing Company Penn Gold

Poached Salmon
WITH CAPER SAUCE

The secret is not to overcook the steaks when poaching. Keep a close eye on the salmon and you will be rewarded with a delectable meal.

1 cup chicken broth

1/4 cup dry white wine

1/8 teaspoon freshly ground black pepper

4 salmon steaks

4 lemon slices

2 tablespoons water

2 teaspoons cornstarch

2 teaspoons drained capers

2 cups shredded zucchini, steamed until tender

In a skillet large enough to hold the salmon steaks, combine the chicken broth, white wine, and pepper. Bring to a simmer over medium heat. Add the salmon steaks and top with a slice of lemon. Cover skillet and simmer for 8 to 12 minutes, or until fish just flakes. Remove salmon with slotted spoon to a platter and keep warm in a 200-degree F oven.

Continue to simmer broth until it is reduced to 3/4 cup. In a small bowl, whisk together the water and cornstarch until smooth. Whisk cornstarch mixture into the simmering broth. Stir in the capers, and continue to whisk until sauce is slightly thickened and bubbly. Divide steamed zucchini onto 4 plates. Top each portion with a salmon steak. Spoon sauce over salmon.

Serves 4

 **Serve with Pennsylvania Brewing Company Penn Gold**

Orange Roughy Fillets
WITH YOGURT GLAZE

Orange roughy is a mild flavored white fish. Sole or red snapper may be substituted and will be just as good.

2 pounds orange roughy fillets

Salt and freshly ground white pepper, to taste

$1/2$ cup plain yogurt

$1/4$ cup freshly grated Parmesan cheese

2 tablespoons horseradish

2 tablespoons freshly squeezed lemon juice

1 tablespoon dry mustard

3 tablespoons minced fresh dill

2 tablespoons capers

Preheat oven to 350 degrees F. Lightly oil a 9 x 9-inch baking dish.

Season the orange roughy with salt and white pepper. Place in the prepared baking dish. In a small bowl, whisk together the yogurt, Parmesan, horseradish, lemon juice, and dry mustard. Spread mixture over the top of the fish. Sprinkle with dill and capers. Bake until the fish just flakes.

Serves 4

Serve with Pennsylvania Brewing Company Penn Gold

Autumn Apple Cake

This cake tastes especially good when the leaves change color and the first cool nights signal the end of summer.

$1^1/_4$ cups sugar

$^1/_2$ cup canola oil

2 egg whites

1 egg

2 teaspoons vanilla extract

1 cup apple juice

$2^3/_4$ cups all-purpose flour

2 teaspoons baking powder

2 teaspoons cinnamon

1 teaspoon nutmeg

$^1/_2$ teaspoon baking soda

3 cups peeled, cored, and diced Granny Smith apples

$^1/_2$ cup chopped walnuts

Preheat oven to 350 degrees F. Butter and flour a 10-inch tube or bundt pan.

In a large bowl, beat together the sugar, canola oil, egg whites, egg, and vanilla extract until creamy. Stir in the apple juice. In a separate bowl, stir together the flour, baking powder, cinnamon, nutmeg, and baking soda until blended. Stir the flour mixture into the creamed mixture and blend until smooth. Gently stir in the apples and walnuts. Pour batter into the prepared pan. Bake for 60 to 65 minutes, or until a toothpick inserted in the center comes out clean.

Serves 12

Serve with Pennsylvania Brewing Company Weizen

Crab Fritters with Roasted Red Pepper Mayonnaise

Executive chef Daniel Dooley proves that you don't have to go to Baltimore to get good crab cakes.

Roasted Red Pepper Mayonnaise:

1 roasted red bell pepper, chopped

2 tablespoons freshly squeezed lemon juice

2 cloves garlic, minced

$1/8$ teaspoon cayenne

1 cup mayonnaise

Salt and freshly ground black pepper, to taste

1 cup all-purpose flour

$1/2$ teaspoon salt

$3/4$ cup Pennsylvania Brewing Company Pilsner, at room temperature

2 egg yolks

2 tablespoons olive oil

2 egg whites

12 ounces fresh crabmeat, picked through for shells

Corn oil or peanut oil for deep-frying

For the mayonnaise: In the bowl of a food processor, combine the roasted pepper, lemon juice, garlic, and cayenne and process until smooth. Add the mayonnaise, salt, and pepper and process until blended. Cover and chill for 1 hour to allow flavors to marry.

In a large bowl, sift together the flour and salt. Add the beer, egg yolks, and olive oil and whisk until smooth. Cover and let stand at room temperature for 1 hour.

In a separate bowl, beat the egg whites until stiff. Gently fold the egg whites and crabmeat into the batter.

In a deep skillet, pour in oil to a depth of 2 inches. Heat to 375 degrees F. Working in batches, drop the crab mixture by heaping tablespoonfuls into the hot oil; do not crowd. Fry, turning often, until golden brown on both sides. With a slotted

(continued on next page)

spoon, transfer fritters to paper towels to drain. Arrange the hot fritters on a platter and serve with the mayonnaise.

Serves 6

 **Serve with Pennsylvania Brewing Company Pilsner**

Give me a woman who loves beer and I will conquer the world.

Kaiser Wilhelm

Pizza Port

Born out of the conviction that pizza is the staff of life and reared on the healthy thirst that naturally follows a great pepperoni, the folks at Pizza Port, a.k.a. Solano Beach Brewery, spent two years planning, licensing, and getting the permits to operate their seven barrel brewery. Located in a corner of their renowned Solano Beach establishment, they recently celebrated their tenth anniversary of making great beers. This is definitely not your average chain pizzeria, and the beer served is no industrial lager. Only fine malts, fresh hops, yeast, and water are used for their beers, except, of course, for the fresh fruit that goes into their fruit ales, because no extracts or syrups ever find their way into their fermenters.

Seafood Chili

*This recipe is a great California version
of this perennial favorite.*

2 tablespoons vegetable oil

1 red onion, chopped

1 white onion, chopped

1 red bell pepper, chopped

1 Anaheim chile, finely chopped

1 jalapeño chile, finely chopped

4 cloves garlic, minced

1/4 cup minced cilantro

1 tablespoon chili powder

1 teaspoon cumin

1 teaspoon oregano

1/4 teaspoon cayenne

1 pound tomatoes, peeled, seeded, and chopped

1/2 cup dry white wine

1 teaspoon green salsa

Salt and freshly ground black pepper, to taste

8 ounces red snapper, cut into 1-inch pieces

8 ounces scallops

8 ounces shrimp

2 pounds live clams

Sour cream, for garnish

Grated cheddar cheese, for garnish

In a large pot, heat the oil over medium heat. Add the red onion, white onion, red bell pepper, Anaheim chile, and jalapeño chile and sauté until onions are translucent. Add the garlic and cilantro and sauté until fragrant. Stir in the chili powder, cumin, oregano, and cayenne and sauté until well mixed. Stir in the tomatoes, wine, and green salsa and simmer until thick. Season with salt and pepper. Gently stir in the fish, scallops, and shrimp and simmer until barely cooked through. Stir in the live clams, cover pot, and simmer for about 3 minutes until clams open. Discard any unopened clams. Divide into 6 bowls and serve with a dollop of sour cream and a sprinkle of cheddar cheese over each portion.

Serves 6

Serve with Pizza Port Palapa Pale Ale

Deep Dish Pizza WITH Spinach and Italian Sausages

Move over Chicago! This version of deep dish pizza will make you crave a second pitcher.

Dough:

1 cup warm water

1 package active dry yeast

1 tablespoon sugar

$1/2$ teaspoon salt

3 to $31/2$ cups bread flour

Filling:

1 package (10 ounces) frozen spinach, thawed and squeezed dry

$3/4$ cup ricotta cheese

$1/2$ cup canned artichoke hearts in brine, drained and chopped

4 ounces (about $3/4$ cup) provolone cheese, grated

4 ounces (about $3/4$ cup) Canadian bacon, diced

2 ounces (about $1/2$ cup) pepperoni, diced

2 ounces (about $1/2$ cup) salami, diced

$1/4$ cup sun-dried tomatoes packed in oil, drained and minced

$1/4$ cup freshly grated Parmesan cheese

1 tablespoon minced garlic

1 tablespoon olive oil
1$^{1}/_{2}$ cups mozzarella cheese, grated

Preheat oven to 350 degrees F. Lightly oil a
9 x 13-inch baking dish.

For the dough: In a large bowl, stir together the
warm water, yeast, and sugar. Let the mixture
stand until foamy. Stir in the salt. Stir in 3 cups
of the bread flour and combine until all of the
liquid is absorbed. If necessary, stir in enough of
the remaining bread flour to form a stiff dough.
Turn dough out onto a lightly floured surface
and knead until dough is smooth and satiny,
about 10 minutes. Place the dough in a lightly
oiled bowl and turn to coat. Cover with a damp
towel and let rise in a warm spot until doubled
in size, about 1$^{1}/_{2}$ hours.

(continued on next page)

Punch the dough down and knead a few times on a lightly floured surface. Cut off $^2/_3$ of the dough and roll out to fit into and up the sides of the prepared baking dish

For the filling: In a large bowl, stir together the spinach, ricotta cheese, artichoke hearts, provolone, Canadian bacon, pepperoni, salami, sun-dried tomatoes, Parmesan, and garlic until well combined. Spread mixture into the bottom of the dough-lined baking dish. Roll out the reserved dough and fit over the top of the filling. Pinch to seal the dough together. Brush the top with olive oil. Let the dough rise for 15 minutes.

Bake the deep dish pizza for 25 minutes. Remove the pizza from oven and sprinkle the top with mozzarella. Return pizza to the oven and bake an additional 25 to 30 minutes, or until the crust is golden brown.

Serves 8

 **Serve with Pizza Port Palapa Pale Ale**

Prescott Brewing Company

When the hot pavement burns the rubber off your shoes and thirst becomes a torment, leave the circling vultures to the blazing sun and stop at the Prescott Brewing Company for a pint of cool beer and filling grub. Arizona's most awarded brewery is also Arizona's friendliest. Located on the historic Courthouse Square in Prescott, their restaurant offers up everything from fish and chips, burgers, steaks, pastas, to everything in between. A wide range of old-fashioned, brewery-fresh non-alcoholic sodas round out a menu diverse enough to satisfy everyone. Next time you find yourself in or passing through Arizona, make a detour to the town of Prescott for a pint of exceptional ale.

Brewer's Cottage Pie

The next time you make mashed potatoes, make extra for this savory pie.

2 pounds potatoes, peeled and quartered

1/4 cup butter, divided

2 tablespoons cream

Salt and freshly ground black pepper, to taste

3 tablespoons olive oil

1 carrot, sliced

1 onion, chopped

4 ounces (about 1 cup) mushrooms, sliced

3 cloves garlic, minced

1 pound sirloin, cut into 1-inch cubes

1/2 cup Prescott Brewing Company Brown Porter

1/2 cup dry red wine

1/4 cup beef stock

1 teaspoon herbes de Provence

2 tablespoons all-purpose flour

1 9-inch prebaked pie shell

Paprika

 Preheat oven to 350 degrees F.

Cook the potatoes in boiling salted water until very tender. Drain, then mash the potatoes with

2 tablespoons of the butter, the cream, salt, and pepper. Set aside.

In a pot, heat the olive oil over medium-high heat. Add the carrot, onion, and mushrooms and sauté until tender. Add the garlic and sauté until fragrant. Add the beef and sauté until browned on all sides. Stir in the porter, wine, beef stock, herbes de Provence, salt, and pepper. Reduce heat to medium-low and simmer, uncovered, for 45 minutes. In a small bowl, blend the remaining 2 tablespoons of butter with the flour until smooth. Stir into the beef mixture and simmer until thickened.

Pour the beef mixture into the pie shell. Top with the reserved mashed potatoes, covering the filling completely. Sprinkle with paprika. Bake for 20 minutes, or until the top is lightly browned. Remove from oven and let cool slightly before cutting.

Serves 6

 **Serve with Prescott Brewing Company Brown Porter**

Pyramid Brewing
Company

In 1984, in the small town of Kalama, Washington, where loggers still stump into bars in their caulk boots and demand a thirst quenching beer, Pyramid Ales was born. Originally known as the Hart Brewing Company, Pyramid Ales quickly became a Northwest favorite and now has breweries in downtown Seattle and Berkeley. This is definitely a beer company you can trust, for the folks at Pyramid state that their mission is to: "Create world-class beers using only classic natural ingredients." All Pyramid ales are shipped unpasteurized for maximum flavor.

Achiote-Marinated Chicken
WITH CORN AND BLACK BEAN SALSA

*Achiote is a paste made from the achiote
seeds that turns the chicken a beautiful
orange and adds a subtle flavor. It can be
found in Mexican markets. Serve over garlic
mashed potatoes.*

Corn and Black Bean Salsa:

2 cups corn

1 1/2 cups cooked black beans

1 onion, diced

1 green bell pepper, diced

1 red bell pepper, diced

1/4 cup minced fresh cilantro

1 tablespoon minced garlic

1 teaspoon freshly ground black pepper

1 teaspoon salt

1/2 teaspoon chili powder

1/2 teaspoon cumin

(continued on next page)

Achiote Marinade:

1 cup Pyramid Brewing Company Pale Ale

$1/3$ cup orange juice

$1/4$ cup freshly squeezed lemon juice

2 tablespoons minced cilantro

2 tablespoons vegetable oil

1 tablespoon achiote paste

1 tablespoon chili powder

1 tablespoon minced jalapeño chile

1 tablespoon paprika

$11/2$ teaspoons freshly ground black pepper

4 boneless chicken breasts

For the salsa: In a bowl, stir together the corn, black beans, onions, green bell pepper, red bell pepper, cilantro, garlic, pepper, salt, chili powder, and cumin. Cover and chill in the refrigerator overnight.

For the marinade: In a shallow dish just large enough to hold the chicken in a single layer, whisk together the ale, orange juice, lemon juice, cilantro, vegetable oil, achiote paste, chili powder, jalapeño, paprika, and pepper. Place the chicken in the marinade, cover and chill in the refrigerator overnight, turning the chicken once.

Prepare a hot grill. Remove the chicken from the marinade and pat dry. Discard the marinade. Transfer chicken to the grill and cook on both sides until done. Serve with the corn and black bean salsa.

Serves 4

 **Serve with Pyramid Brewing Company Pale Ale**

They who drink beer will think beer.

Washington Irving

Wild Mixed Salad
WITH HAZELNUT VINAIGRETTE

When you feel an overwhelming need for greens, check out this mix! The dressing is simply outstanding and would go with pretty much any combination of salad greens if the more exotic "wild" aren't available.

Hazelnut Vinaigrette:

2 tablespoons freshly squeezed lemon juice

1 tablespoon half-and-half

1 teaspoon Dijon mustard

1 teaspoon minced garlic

1/8 teaspoon cayenne

Salt and freshly ground black pepper, to taste

2 tablespoons hazelnut oil

2/3 cup safflower oil

1/3 cup vegetable oil

6 cups wild mixed greens

1 cup alfalfa sprouts, chopped

1 carrot, julienned

1 cup crumbled feta cheese

For the vinaigrette: In a bowl, whisk together the lemon juice, half-and-half, Dijon mustard, garlic, cayenne, salt, and pepper. Whisk in the hazelnut oil. Whisk in the safflower oil and vegetable oil.

In a large bowl, combine the greens, alfalfa sprouts, and carrots. Pour in the dressing and toss to coat. Divide onto 6 plates. Sprinkle with feta cheese and serve immediately.

Serves 6

Serve with Pyramid Brewing Company Pale Ale

Rock Bottom
Restaurants

Rock Bottom is, first and foremost, known as a restaurant that brews its own beer, rather than a brewery that cooks its own food. That in a nutshell is the key to their success. Over thirty restaurant/breweries nationwide attest to their success in bringing good food and good beer to the public. But more than that, Rock Bottom personifies the Cajun concept of "Lagniappe," a term that means "that extra something special that is all the sweeter because it is unexpected." Each employee has the responsibility to ensure that the customers are entertained and made happy during their time at a Rock Bottom Restaurant. It's often the small things that make for a memorable meal, and at Rock Bottom, that is a virtual guarantee. So the next time you see a Rock Bottom Brewery sign, take the time to stop by and enjoy the hospitality that has made Rock Bottom one of America's fastest growing brewery/restaurants.

Rock Bottom Brown Ale Chicken

Mashed potatoes are the perfect side dish to go with this chicken. The sauce is excellent when poured over a pile of creamy spuds.

Brown Ale Sauce:

Bones from 6 chicken breasts (really!)

1 1/2 cups Rock Bottom Brown Ale

1 cup chicken stock

1/2 cup chopped carrots

1/2 cup chopped celery

1/2 cup chopped onions

1/2 teaspoon malt vinegar

1/2 teaspoon molasses

1/2 teaspoon salt

1/2 teaspoon freshly ground black pepper

1 bay leaf

For the sauce: In a large saucepan, combine the chicken bones, ale, chicken stock, carrots, celery, onions, malt vinegar, molasses,

(continued on next page)

salt, pepper, and bay leaf. Bring to a boil, then reduce heat to medium-low and simmer until liquid is reduced to 1 cup. Strain the sauce and discard the solids. Set sauce aside.

6 chicken breasts, bones removed for sauce

Salt and freshly ground black pepper, to taste

All-purpose flour, for dredging

3 tablespoons vegetable oil

12 ounces fresh shiitake mushrooms, sliced

$1/2$ cup heavy cream

$1/2$ cup cold butter, cut into small pieces

$1/4$ cup thinly sliced scallions, for garnish

For the chicken: Season the chicken breasts with salt and pepper. Dredge lightly in flour and shake off the excess. In a large skillet, heat the oil over medium-high heat. Add the chicken breasts and brown on both sides. Reduce heat to medium and continue to cook until chicken is cooked through. Transfer chicken breasts to a platter and keep warm. Add mushrooms to the skillet and sauté until tender. Whisk in reserved sauce and bring to a simmer. Stir in cream and simmer until liquid is reduced by one-third.

Remove skillet from heat and whisk in the butter, one piece at a time, until it is all incorporated. Spoon sauce over the chicken and sprinkle with scallions.

Serves 6

 **Serve with Rock Bottom Brown Ale**

O Beer! O Hodgson, Guinness, Allsopp, Bass! Names that should be on every infant's tongue.

C. V. Calverley

Rockies Brewing Company

It's quite an honor to be the oldest operating microbrewery in the United States, and the Rockies Brewing Company upholds that honor with distinction. Pure Rockie Mountain glacier water goes into their brews, which contain only the finest, all-natural ingredients. Six year-round ales and three limited edition seasonals comprise their palette of Boulder, Colorado, beers. If you have to catch a special flight, board a special train, or race a special car to Boulder, do so and enjoy one of the Rockies best beers.

Black Pepper Gnocchi WITH ROASTED WILD MUSHROOMS, AGED BALSAMIC VINEGAR, AND COPPER ALE

John Trejo uses 10 to 25-year-old balsamic vinegar for this dish. A bit of a splurge, but well worth it.

4 cups assorted wild mushrooms (shiitake, oyster mushrooms, and chanterelles), sliced in half if large

2 tablespoons olive oil

1^1/2 teaspoons minced garlic

Salt and freshly ground black pepper, to taste

1 cup Rockies Brewing Company Singletrack Copper Ale

2 tablespoons butter

2 tablespoons aged balsamic vinegar

^{1}/2 teaspoon minced fresh thyme

Black Pepper Gnocchi:

2 pounds russet potatoes, peeled and diced

1 egg

1 egg yolk

1 teaspoon freshly ground black pepper

(continued on next page)

1 teaspoon salt

1/4 teaspoon nutmeg

2 1/4 cups all-purpose flour

2 tablespoons olive oil

1 cup grated fresh Parmesan cheese

Minced fresh chives, for garnish

Preheat oven to 400 degrees F. Lightly oil a
9 x 13-inch baking dish.

Place the mushrooms in prepared baking dish.
Add the olive oil, garlic, salt, and pepper and
toss together. Place in the oven and roast for
10 minutes, or until mushrooms are tender and
lightly golden brown. Remove from the oven
and stir in the ale, butter, balsamic vinegar, and
thyme. Set aside.

For the gnocchi: Bring a large pot of salted
water to a boil. Add the potatoes and boil until
tender. Drain thoroughly, then put the potatoes
through a potato ricer or food mill into a large
bowl. In a small bowl, whisk together the egg,
egg yolk, pepper, salt, and nutmeg until well
blended. With a wooden spoon, stir the egg mixture into the potatoes until well blended. Stir in
the flour until you have a stiff dough. Turn out

onto a lightly floured board and knead until smooth, sprinkling with additional flour if the dough sticks. Divide into 6 pieces. Using the palms of your hands, roll each piece into a log about 1 inch in diameter. Cut the logs into 1-inch pieces. Hold the gnocchi and roll along the tines of a fork to create a ridged surface. Arrange them on a lightly floured baking sheet so they do not touch each other.

Bring a large pot of salted water to a boil. Add the gnocchi and cook until they float to the surface. Transfer the gnocchi with a slotted spoon to a colander and drain well.

In a large skillet, heat the olive oil over medium-high heat. Add the drained gnocchi and sauté quickly until golden brown. Add the reserved mushroom mixture and bring to a simmer.

To serve, divide hot gnocchi into 6 bowls. Spoon mushrooms and broth over the gnocchi. Top each portion with Parmesan and chives and serve immediately.

Serves 6

 **Serve with Rockies Brewing Company Singletrack Copper Ale**

Slap Happy Shrimp

If your idea of happiness is a weekend spent with buddies watching a knock-down, drag-out sporting event on the wide-screen TV, then make sure you have a supply of cold beers and a pile of these scrumptious shrimp treats to keep everyone happy.

3/4 cup Rockies Brewing Company Boulder Pale Ale

1 tablespoon vegetable oil

2 teaspoons minced fresh chives

2 cloves garlic, minced

1/2 teaspoon Tabasco sauce

1/4 teaspoon salt

1 pound medium shrimp, shelled and deveined

Melted butter

Lemon wedges

In a large bowl, whisk together the ale, vegetable oil, chives, garlic, Tabasco sauce, and salt. Add the shrimp and toss to coat. Cover and refrigerate 1 to 3 hours.

Preheat the broiler. Remove the shrimp from marinade. Discard the marinade. Place shrimp on the rack in the broiler pan. Broil the shrimp until they have turned pink and are cooked through. Serve with melted butter and lemon wedges.

Serves 6

Serve with Rockies Brewing Company Boulder Pale Ale

Porter Stew

There is something about high altitudes that demands hearty meals. Whether you are trekking in Tibet, chilling in the Andes, or skiing in the Rockies, everyone craves a rich, cozy, satisfying stew. Enjoy this version of Boulder's best.

$2^1/2$ pounds beef stew meat

Salt and freshly ground black pepper, to taste

All-purpose flour, for dredging

$1/3$ cup olive oil, divided

1 onion, chopped

1 rib celery, sliced

1 jalapeño chile, minced

1 tablespoon minced garlic

3 cups Rockies Brewing Company Boulder Porter

3 cups beef stock

1 potato, peeled and chopped

1 cup chopped tomatoes

2 bay leaves

1 teaspoon rosemary

Season the beef with salt and pepper. Dredge lightly in flour and shake off the excess. In a large pot, heat 3 tablespoons of the olive oil. Brown the meat well on all sides. With a slotted spoon, remove the meat to a bowl and set aside. Add the remaining 3 tablespoons olive oil to the pot. Add the onion, celery, and jalapeño and sauté until onion is tender. Add the garlic and sauté until fragrant. Stir in the beer and bring to a simmer. Stir in reserved beef, beef stock, potato, tomatoes, bay leaves, and rosemary and bring to a simmer. Reduce heat to medium-low, cover pot, and simmer until beef is very tender, about 2 hours.

Serves 6 to 8

Serve with Rockies Brewing Company Boulder Porter

Rogue Ales

"For the Rogue in all of us," the motto of Newport, Oregon's Rogue brewery sums up just about everything one needs to know about the brewery. Located where the fishing fleet makes its repairs after slogging through the icy water of the Pacific Northwest, the brewery offers thirsty men what they need. Crystal clear coast range water, aromatic hops, and the finest of barleys are the ingredients in its distinctive and thirst-quenching brews. When you feel the need to reach back to your roots and be a rogue, there is only one beer you need to grab.

Ale-Battered Fish

Folks who live on the coast know how to treat fish right. This recipe proves the folks in Newport, Oregon, know their fish.

1³/₄ cups all-purpose flour

1 teaspoon dill

1 teaspoon Mrs. Dash seasoning or Spike seasoning

2 teaspoons baking powder

1 cup water

¹/₃ cup Rogue Ales YSB Ale

1 egg

2 pounds cod or other mild fish, cut into 6 serving
  pieces

Oil for deep frying

In a large bowl, combine the flour, dill, seasoning mix, and baking powder. Stir with a fork until blended. Add the water, ale, and egg and whisk until smooth.

(continued on next page)

In a deep fryer, heat oil to 375 degrees F. Dip the fish into the batter, allowing excess to drip off. Carefully place fish into hot oil and cook until deep golden brown on all sides. With a slotted spoon, remove fish and drain briefly on paper towels. Serve very hot.

Serves 6

 Serve with Rogue Ales YSB Ale

Life ain't all beer and skittles, and more's the pity.

George DuMaurier

Brutal Bitter Rueben Sandwich

The only bitter thing about this sandwich is the feeling you get when it's gone. Time to grill another!

2^1/$_2$ pounds corned beef

3 cups Rogue Ales Brutal Bitter Ale

2 cups water

1 lemon, cut into wedges

16 slices rye bread

1 cup thousand island dressing

1 pound sauerkraut, drained

8 slices Swiss cheese

Dill pickles, for garnish

In a pot just large enough to hold the corned beef, combine the corned beef, ale, water, and lemon wedges. Bring to a boil, then reduce heat to medium-low, cover the pot, and simmer for 3 hours. Drain the corned beef and transfer to a cutting board. Slice thinly across

(continued on next page)

 **185**

the grain. Spread thousand island dressing on the rye bread. Arrange the corned beef onto 8 slices of the rye bread. Divide the sauerkraut on top of meat and top with a piece of Swiss cheese. Top with remaining rye bread. Grill in a hot skillet until golden brown on both sides. Serve with dill pickles on the side.

Serves 8

 **Serve with Rogue Ales**
Brutal Bitter Ale

If all be true that I do think,
There are five reasons
we should drink:
Good beer—a friend—or being dry—
Or lest we should be by and by—
Or any other reason why.

Anon.

Russian River Brewing Company

Born of the need for wine folks to quench their thirst during the long hot grape harvest, the Russian River Brewing Company is housed at two different and separate wineries in the wine-growing region of Sonoma County. The historic Korbel Champagne Cellars in Guerneville, on the road to the coast from Healdsburg, houses the original brewhouse, and the second facility is at Lake Sonoma Winery at the north end of the Dry Creek Valley, also just west of Healdsburg. Brewers since 1997, they offer four year-round beers plus an additional rotating seasonal beer as well. One of the unique aspects of this brewery is the hops that are planted at each facility. They are hand-picked and used in a special brew called "HopTime Harvest Ale." In this distinctive beer, more than six times the standard amount of hops are used. This eagerly anticipated beer is released every September.

Beer and Cheese Soup
WITH CROUTONS

*Linda Kittler, wine country chef extraordin-
aire, has used her talents to create this
extraordinary country beer soup.*

Croutons:

3 tablespoons olive oil, plus more if necessary

4 slices day old French bread, 1 inch thick

Beer and Cheese Soup:

1 cup grated cheddar cheese

1/2 cup grated Monterey Jack cheese

1 tablespoon cornstarch

2 tablespoons butter

1 cup finely diced onions

1 tablespoon minced serrano chile

1 teaspoon dried thyme leaves

1/2 teaspoon freshly ground black pepper

2 cups chicken stock

1 cup Russian River Brewing Company Golden
  Wheat Ale

1/2 teaspoon salt, or to taste

1/4 teaspoon liquid smoke flavoring

1/4 cup grated Asiago cheese

For the croutons: In a skillet, heat the olive oil over medium heat. Add the bread and sauté until browned and crisp on both sides, adding a little more oil if necessary. Drain on paper towels and set aside.

For the soup: In a bowl, toss together the cheddar cheese, Jack cheese, and cornstarch. Set aside. In a large saucepan, melt the butter over medium heat. Add the onions, chile, thyme, and black pepper and sauté, stirring occasionally, until the onions are translucent. Stir in the chicken stock, ale, salt, and liquid smoke. Bring to a simmer and remove from heat. Gently stir reserved cheese mixture into the soup. Divide the croutons into the bottom of 4 deep soup bowls. Ladle soup over the bread. Garnish each portion with 1 tablespoon Asiago cheese and serve immediately.

Serves 4

Serve with Russian River Brewing Company Golden Wheat Ale

Sierra Nevada Brewing Company

A true local beer, Sierra Nevada is one of the pillars of the farming town of Chico, California, in the northern Sierra foothills. Locally owned, with beers locally brewed, and definitely locally enjoyed, Sierra Nevada is one brewery that does not advertise on either radio or television. Their marketing policy is fundamental and practical: Create a superior product, it will sell itself and business will boom. Sierra Nevada Brewing Company is proof of the wisdom of this simple theory. Chico chemistry student Ken Grossman and his friend Paul Camusi founded the brewery in 1980, and have been running at full speed ever since. The beer is currently available in all 50 states and Sierra is currently the 15th largest beer-producing company in the United States.

Ale-Marinated Flank Steak

The marinating breaks down and tenderizes an otherwise tough piece of meat.

Ale Marinade:

$1/2$ cup packed brown sugar

1 onion, chopped

3 cloves garlic, chopped

2 tablespoons olive oil

1 tablespoon soy sauce

1 tablespoon Worcestershire sauce

$1/2$ teaspoon garlic powder

$1/2$ teaspoon salt

$1/4$ teaspoon freshly ground black pepper

$1 1/2$ cups Sierra Nevada Brewing Company Pale Ale

$1 1/2$ pounds flank steak

For the marinade: In a blender or the bowl of a food processor, combine brown sugar, onion, garlic, olive oil, soy sauce, Worcestershire

(continued on next page)

sauce, garlic powder, salt, and pepper and process until smooth. In a saucepan, combine the brown sugar mixture and ale. Bring to a boil over high heat, then reduce heat to medium-low and simmer for 5 minutes. Pour into a shallow dish and let cool.

With a sharp knife, lightly score the flank steak with a diamond pattern on both sides. Place the meat in the marinade, cover, and refrigerate overnight, turning several times.

Prepare a hot charcoal fire. Remove the flank steak from the marinade and grill on both sides until medium-rare, about 10 minutes. Transfer the steak to a cutting board and let rest 5 minutes before carving. Thinly slice the meat across the grain and serve.

Serves 6

Serve with Sierra Nevada Brewing Company Pale Ale

Welsh Rarebit

This is a classy version of a classic. Perfect for a small party.

3 tablespoons butter

3 tablespoons all-purpose flour

$^2/_3$ cup Sierra Nevada Brewing Company Pale Ale

1 pound tomatoes, finely chopped

1 teaspoon Dijon mustard

1 teaspoon Worcestershire sauce

$^1/_4$ teaspoon Tabasco sauce

10 ounces (about $1^1/_2$ cups) extra-sharp cheddar cheese, grated

6 thick slices French bread, lightly toasted

8 ounces (about 1 cup) bacon, crisply cooked and crumbled

3 tablespoons chopped parsley

In a large saucepan, melt the butter over medium heat. Whisk in the flour until bubbly. Whisk in the ale and simmer until slightly thickened. Add the tomatoes and simmer, stirring often, until slightly thickened. Whisk in the

(continued on next page)

mustard, Worcestershire sauce, and Tabasco sauce until blended. Reduce heat to medium-low and stir in the cheese until melted. Divide the toasted French bread onto 6 plates. Divide the cheese sauce on top of the French bread. Sprinkle with bacon and parsley and serve immediately.

Serve 6

Serve with Sierra Nevada Brewing Company Pale Ale

*You foam within our glasses,
you lusty golden brew,
whoever imbibes takes fire from you.
The young and the old sing your
praises; here's to beer, here's to cheer,
here's to beer.*

A toast in Bedrich Smetana's 1866 opera *The Bartered Bride*

Taproom Pizza

There is something fundamentally satisfying about good beer and good pizza. Give both a try with this recipe and a pint of Sierra Nevada.

1 14-inch unbaked pizza crust

2 tablespoons olive oil

3 tablespoons roasted garlic, chopped

3 tablespoons butter

12 ounces (about 2 cups) fresh spinach, chopped

12 ounces (about 2 cups) mushrooms, sliced

8 ounces (about 1 cup) fontina cheese, grated

8 ounces (about 1 cup) mozzarella cheese, grated

 Preheat oven to 350 degrees F.

Place pizza crust on a baking sheet. Brush with the olive oil, then sprinkle with roasted garlic, and set aside.

In a large skillet, melt the butter over medium-high heat. Add the spinach and sauté until wilted. With a slotted spoon, remove spinach

(continued on next page)

and sprinkle over the pizza crust. Add the mushrooms to the skillet and sauté until very tender and almost all of the liquid has evaporated. Sprinkle mushrooms over the spinach. Sprinkle cheeses over the pizza. Bake for about 20 minutes, or until the crust is golden brown and the cheese is bubbly.

Serves 4 to 6

 **Serve with Sierra Nevada Brewing Company Pale Ale**

Silverado Brewing Company

On your next trip to the wine country, wash away the dust of the Napa Valley with a visit to the Silverado Brewing Company. Located at the historic Freemark Abbey Winery, north of St. Helena, California, the brewery was founded in September of 2000 with the slogan, "It takes a lot of great beer to make good wine." The able-bodied Ken Mee brews an assortment of ales and lagers in the brewery whose walls date back to the 1800s. Sit at the bar and gaze longingly at the gleaming copper and stainless brewery or slip into the restaurant and dine on one of the specialties of the house, and you might just find yourself telling the rest of your friends to go on wine tasting without you.

Mussels Steamed in Oktoberfest Ale

As long as man has been around, mussels have been gathered from the sea and enjoyed. "Gather" some of your favorite fresh mussels from your local fish market and enjoy!

1/4 cup butter

2 tablespoons olive oil

1 tablespoon finely minced shallots

1 tablespoon chopped garlic

6 ounces (about 1 cup) andouille sausage, finely diced

1 cup chopped fresh spinach

1 cup diced tomatoes

1 tablespoon minced fresh basil

1 tablespoon minced fresh parsley

1 1/2 cups vegetable stock

1/2 cup Silverado Brewing Company Oktoberfest Ale

Salt and freshly ground black pepper, to taste

3 pounds mussels, scrubbed and debearded

In a large pot, heat the butter and olive oil over medium heat. Add the shallots and garlic and sauté until fragrant. Stir in the sausage and spinach and sauté until spinach has completely wilted. Stir in the tomatoes, basil, and parsley and sauté for 3 minutes. Stir in the vegetable stock, ale, salt, and pepper. Increase heat to high and bring to a boil. Add the mussels, cover, and steam for about 3 minutes until the mussels open. Transfer mussels to a large serving bowl. Discard any mussels that do not open. Pour broth over the mussels and serve.

Serves 6

Serve with Silverado Brewing Company Oktoberfest Ale

Pear and Butternut Squash Soup WITH AMBER ALE

Try this tangy combination of tree-ripened pears and creamy squash.

2 tablespoons butter

1 cup chopped onions

1 tablespoon minced fresh ginger

2 cups chicken stock

$1^{1}/_{2}$ cups Silverado Brewing Company Amber Ale

3 pounds butternut squash, peeled and cubed

1 pear, peeled and diced

$^{1}/_{4}$ teaspoon cinnamon

$^{1}/_{4}$ teaspoon nutmeg

$^{1}/_{4}$ teaspoon vanilla extract

Salt and freshly ground black pepper, to taste

In a large pot, melt the butter over medium heat. Add the onion and sauté until translucent. Add the ginger and sauté until fragrant. Add the chicken stock and ale and bring to a simmer. Stir in the butternut squash, pear, cinnamon, nutmeg, and vanilla and bring to a simmer. Reduce heat to medium-low, cover the pot, and simmer until squash is very tender, about 1 hour. Purée the soup in batches and return to the pot. Season with salt and pepper and heat through.

Serves 8

Serve with Silverado Brewing Company Amber Ale

Lamb Shanks Braised in Oatmeal Stout

Great over mashed potatoes. Just let the gravy work its magic on the spuds.

4 lamb shanks

Salt and freshly ground black pepper, to taste

1/4 cup olive oil

1 cup chopped onions

1/4 cup chopped celery

3 cloves garlic

2 cups Silverado Brewing Company Oatmeal Stout

2 cups chicken stock

 Preheat oven to 400 degrees F.

Season lamb shanks with salt and pepper. In a large pot, heat the olive oil over medium-high heat. Add the lamb and brown well on all sides. Add the onions, celery, and garlic and sauté until the onions are translucent. Add the stout and bring to a simmer. Add the chicken stock and bring to a simmer. Cover the pot and place in the oven for $1^1/2$ hours, or until lamb shanks are very tender. Remove from oven and transfer lamb shanks to a platter and keep warm.

Place the pot over medium heat and simmer until liquid is reduced by half. Strain the sauce through a sieve and discard solids. Season the sauce with salt and pepper and pour over the lamb shanks.

Serves 4

Serve with Silverado Brewing Company Oatmeal Stout

South Hampton
Public House

It is worth the trip to New York's Long Island to sample the unique beers brewed by Phil Markowski. Among his offerings is the only beer I am aware of that combines locally-grown Chardonnay grapes with two-row barley. The Peconic County Reserve is an unusual ale that borrows on ingredients from the world's most popular white wine. In addition to the Peconic County Reserve, South Hampton brews a range of beers in the British, German, American, and Belgian styles.

Poached Salmon and Marinated Eggplant Salad WITH ROASTED RED PEPPER RELISH

The combination of flavors and textures in this recipe are truly unique, so when you're looking for inspiration the next time you have a nice piece of salmon, try this recipe.

Roasted Red Pepper Relish:

1 roasted red bell pepper, chopped

1 small red onion, chopped

$1/2$ cup black olives, chopped

1 tablespoon sugar

1 tablespoon distilled vinegar

$1/2$ teaspoon Dijon mustard

Marinated Eggplant:

1 cup olive oil

$1/2$ cup balsamic vinegar

1 tablespoon chopped garlic

1 teaspoon basil

(continued on next page)

1 teaspoon oregano

1 teaspoon thyme

1 large eggplant, peeled and julienned

2 cups South Hampton Public House
   Montaulk Light Beer

1 pound salmon filet

For the relish: In a bowl, combine the roasted pepper, red onion, olives, sugar, vinegar, and mustard and stir until sugar dissolves. Cover and let stand for 1 hour to allow flavors to marry.

For the eggplant: In a bowl, whisk together the olive oil, vinegar, garlic, basil, oregano, and thyme. Add the julienned eggplant and toss gently to coat.

In a skillet, bring the beer to a simmer over medium heat. Add the salmon and poach until fish just begins to flake. Transfer fish to a cutting board and cut into 4 serving pieces. Divide the marinated eggplant onto 4 plates. Top with a piece of salmon and spoon relish over the salmon.

Serves 4

 **Serve with South Hampton Public House Montaulk Light Beer**

Let us sing our own treasures,
Old England's good cheer,
To the profits and pleasures of stout
British beer;
Your wine tippling, dram sipping
fellows retreat,
But your beer drinking Britons can
never be beat.
The French with their vineyards
and meager pale ale,
They drink from the squeezing
of half ripe fruit;
But we, who have hop-yards
to mellow our ale,
Are rosy and plump and have
freedom to boot.

English drinking song, circa 1757

Stoudt Brewing Company

The Stoudt Brewing Company is Pennsylvania's first true microbrewery since Prohibition. It was founded by the first female brewmaster in America since Prohibition, Carol Stoudt, who has been a pioneer in the craft brewing industry for over thirteen years. Stoudt's philosophy is to brew a quality beer with all natural ingredients and no preservatives for the freshest possible taste.

Stoudt's Famous Cheese Spread

This is the house cheese spread served at the Stoudt's Black Angus Restaurant. Be warned, once you start, it's hard to stop! Fresh herbs or caraway can be added if desired.

10 ounces cream cheese, at room temperature

8 ounces Camembert or Brie cheese, diced

1 onion, finely chopped

1^1/$_2$ tablespoons butter, softened

1 teaspoon paprika

1 tablespoon Stoudt Brewing Company Fest Lager

Salt and freshly ground black pepper, to taste

In the bowl of a food processor, combine all ingredients and process until smooth. Transfer to a serving dish, cover, and refrigerate for 3 hours to allow flavors to marry. Serve with bread or crackers.

Serves 8 to 10

 **Serve with Stoudt Brewing Company Fest Lager**

Beer-Boiled Mussels and Bratwurst

This is a beerhouse version of "surf and turf," and a perfect companion for a mug of the frostiest.

2 tablespoons butter

4 ounces bratwurst sausage, chopped

$1/2$ cup diced red bell pepper

1 leek, white and pale green part only, chopped

2 cloves garlic, minced

$1^1/2$ cups Stoudt Brewing Company Gold Lager

$1^1/2$ cups water

1 teaspoon salt

$1/2$ teaspoon freshly ground black pepper

3 dozen mussels, scrubbed and debearded

In a large pot, melt the butter over medium heat. Add the bratwurst and sauté until golden brown. Add the red bell pepper, leek, and garlic and sauté until fragrant. Stir in the beer, water, salt, and pepper. Bring to a boil over medium-high heat and simmer for 3 minutes. Increase heat to high and bring to a boil. Add the mussels, cover, and steam for about 3 minutes until mussels open. Transfer mussels to a large serving bowl and discard any that do not open. Pour broth over mussels and serve.

Serves 4

Serve with Stoudt Brewing Company Gold Lager

OATMEAL STOUT

Titanic Brewing Company

Kevin Rusk, proprietor of the Titanic Brewing Company, is a beer aficionado who turned a passion for brewing into the most successful brewpub in South Florida. He recognized early on, however, the importance of good food in a pub's success, and planned accordingly. His restaurant packs the people in and is the pillar on which the success of the Titanic is based. But that doesn't mean that the beers are anything short of spectacular. His customers are educated and discriminating and would not settle for anything less. From his Brewmaster dinners to his "Stout and Stogie" nights, Kevin offers patrons an outstanding night on the town. This time the Titanic definitely has made it to port.

Gangplank Cedar Salmon

The idea of cooking a salmon on a cedar plank comes from the extreme other corner of the country: the Pacific Northwest. This Florida restaurant has taken a good idea and added a distinctly Caribbean twist. When you go to your local hardware store or lumber yard to get your plank, be sure it hasn't been treated with any chemicals.

Cedar plank large enough to hold the salmon

1 orange, quartered

3/4 cup freshly squeezed orange juice

1/2 cup molasses

1/4 cup dark rum

2 tablespoons minced fresh ginger

2 tablespoons ketchup

2 tablespoons soy sauce

1 tablespoon balsamic vinegar

1 1/2 teaspoons minced garlic

1 salmon fillet, about 2 pounds, skinned and small bones removed

(continued on next page)

 Place cedar plank in a container large enough to submerge it and cover with water. Place quartered orange in the container with the cedar plank. Soak for 2 hours.

Preheat oven to 400 degrees F.

In a saucepan, stir together the orange juice, molasses, rum, ginger, ketchup, soy sauce, balsamic vinegar, and garlic and bring to a boil over medium heat. Reduce heat to medium-low and simmer until thickened and syrupy. Set aside.

Remove cedar plank from the water and place salmon on top. Brush salmon thickly with the glaze. Place in the oven and roast for about 20 minutes, or until the fish just flakes. Serve immediately.

Serves 6

Serve with Titanic Brewing Company White Star India Pale Ale

S.O.S. Grilled Shrimp

Three short shrimps, three long drinks, then three short shrimps again are the true meaning of the international signal of S.O.S. Serve these at your next tailgater.

2 ounces (about $1/4$ cup) almonds

$1/4$ cup cilantro

$1/4$ cup vegetable oil

$1/3$ cup water

4 scallions, chopped

1 jalapeño chile, seeded

3 cloves garlic

1 tablespoon cumin

24 large shrimp

2 limes, for garnish

In the bowl of a food processor, combine the almonds, cilantro, vegetable oil, water, scallions, jalapeño, garlic, and cumin. Process until smooth. Pour marinade into a shallow dish.

(continued on next page)

Thread 4 shrimp onto each of the 6 skewers. Place in the marinade and turn to coat. Cover and chill in refrigerator for 1 hour.

Prepare a hot grill. Grill shrimp on both sides until they turn pink. Serve with lime wedges.

Serves 6

 **Serve with Titanic Brewing Company Hurricane Reef Pilsner**

Beer makes you feel the way you ought to feel without beer.

Henry Lawson

Trap Rock Brewery

Just walk through the doors of the Trap Rock Restaurant and Brewery and leave the bustle of North Central New Jersey behind. The brewpub offers the ambience of an English country inn and serves up a blend of classical American and French cuisine, exceptional beer styles, and impeccable service. More and more, folks on the East Coast are discovering how pleasant an experience a night spent with simple and tasty food, a mug of cool beer, and good friends can be.

Pan-Seared Squid WITH THAI CHILI PASTE

If it's not available at your supermarket,
check out an Asian market for the chili paste.

1 pound squid, sliced into rings

Salt and freshly ground black pepper, to taste

1/4 cup olive oil

1 tablespoon chili paste

2 teaspoons chopped garlic

2 teaspoons chopped shallots

1 cup shredded napa cabbage

1 cup peas

3 tablespoons freshly squeezed lemon juice

1 tablespoon chopped fresh mint

Season the squid with salt and pepper. In a large skillet, heat the olive oil over high heat. Add the squid and stir-fry until lightly seared but not cooked through. Add the chili paste, garlic, and shallots and stir-fry until fragrant. Add the cabbage and stir-fry until crisp-tender. Stir in the peas and lemon juice. Divide onto 4 plates and sprinkle with the mint.

Serves 4

Serve with Trap Rock Brewery Pale Ale

Lobster with Sugar Snap Peas and Rice Noodles
WITH MANGO VINAIGRETTE

Try this sweet-sour-tangy specialty when you want to serve something to wow your guests.

1 cup mango purée

$1/4$ cup rice wine vinegar

1 tablespoon minced shallots

1 tablespoon sugar

$1/4$ cup olive oil

Salt and freshly ground black pepper, to taste

4 ounces rice noodles, cooked in boiling salted water until tender, then drained

2 cooked lobster tails, shelled and sliced

4 ounces sugar snap peas, blanched for 1 minute in boiling water, then drained

 In a large bowl, whisk together the mango purée, rice wine vinegar, shallots, and sugar until the sugar dissolves. Whisk in the olive oil, salt, and pepper. Add the drained rice noodles to the mango vinaigrette and toss lightly. Divide noodles onto 4 plates. Arrange lobster sliced on top and fan the sugar snap peas decoratively around the edge of the plates.

Serves 4

 **Serve with Trap Rock Brewery Rising Sun Wheat Beer**

Grilled Tuna WITH Harissa Rub, Kalamata Olive Cous Cous, Yellow Tomato Vinaigrette, AND Vidalia Onion Relish

Harissa is a fiery Middle Eastern chile paste that can be found in specialty and Middle Eastern markets.

Vidalia Onion Relish:

1 cup thinly sliced Vidalia onions

1 teaspoon chopped fresh mint

1 teaspoon sugar

1 teaspoon rice vinegar

Salt and freshly ground black pepper, to taste

Yellow Tomato Vinaigrette:

1 yellow tomato, peeled, seeded, and puréed

1/4 cup white wine

2 tablespoons olive oil

2 tablespoons sherry vinegar

1/2 teaspoon sugar

Salt and freshly ground black pepper, to taste

Kalamata Olive Cous Cous:

2 cups chicken stock

1/4 cup olive oil

1/4 cup chopped kalamata olives

1 cup cous cous

4 tuna steaks

Salt and freshly ground black pepper, to taste

2 tablespoons harissa

 **For the relish:** In a small bowl, combine the onions, mint, sugar, rice vinegar, salt, and black pepper. Set aside.

(continued on next page)

For the vinaigrette: In a bowl, whisk together the tomato purée, white wine, olive oil, sherry vinegar, sugar, salt, and pepper until smooth. Set aside.

For the cous cous: In a saucepan, stir together the chicken stock, olive oil, and olives. Bring the mixture to a boil. Whisk in the cous cous, cover the saucepan, and remove from heat. Let stand for 10 minutes.

Prepare a hot grill. Season tuna steaks with salt and pepper. Brush both sides of each steak with harissa. Grill quickly on both sides. (Tuna should be rare!)

Divide cous cous onto 4 plates. Top with a tuna steak. Drizzle vinaigrette around the plates. Sprinkle with the onion relish.

Serves 4

 **Serve with Trap Rock Brewery Hathor Red**

Pork Chops Wrapped in Prosciutto WITH Cous Cous AND Peach Compote

If there were a signature dish for Trap Rock, this would have to be it.

Peach Compote:

1 tablespoon canola oil

2 peaches, peeled and chopped

$1/4$ cup honey

$1/4$ cup sherry vinegar

1 cinnamon stick

1 bay leaf

Salt and freshly ground black pepper, to taste

Cous Cous:

2 tablespoons canola oil

1 onion, finely chopped

2 ribs celery, finely chopped

1 carrot, finely chopped

$1^1/2$ cups cous cous

1 teaspoon minced fresh rosemary

(continued on next page)

1 teaspoon minced fresh thyme

1/2 teaspoon ground coriander

2 cups chicken stock

1/2 cup fresh fava beans

1/2 cup chopped tomatoes

1 1/2 teaspoons minced fresh tarragon

Salt and freshly ground black pepper, to taste

Pork Chops Wrapped with Prosciutto:

4 (6 ounces each) boneless pork chops

Salt and freshly ground black pepper, to taste

8 fresh sage leaves

4 slices prosciutto

2 tablespoons canola oil

Preheat oven to 375 degrees F. Lightly oil a broiling pan.

For the peach compote: In a saucepan, heat the oil over medium heat. Add the peaches, honey, vinegar, cinnamon stick, and bay leaf and simmer until mixture is reduced by half. Season with salt and pepper and set aside.

For the cous cous: In a large saucepan, heat the oil over medium-high heat. Add the onion, celery, and carrot and sauté until tender. Stir in the cous cous, rosemary, thyme, and coriander. Stir in the chicken stock and bring to a boil. Reduce heat to low, cover, and simmer 10 minutes. Stir in the fava beans, tomatoes, tarragon, salt, and pepper. Set aside and keep warm.

For the pork chops: Season pork chops with salt and pepper. Place 2 sage leaves on each pork chop, then wrap with prosciutto. Secure with a toothpick. In a skillet, heat oil over high heat. Place the pork chops in the skillet and sear on both sides. Transfer pork chops to the prepared broiling pan. Cook for 12 to 15 minutes, or until done.

Divide cous cous onto 4 plates. Top with a pork chop and spoon the peach compote on top.

Serves 4

 **Serve with Trap Rock Brewery Hathor Red**

Triple 7 Restaurant and Brewery

Las Vegas is home not only to miles of neon, shiny low-riders, and dreams of instant wealth, but also to one of the newest and most exciting breweries in America. Live music composed of "dueling concert grand pianos," a raw bar featuring freshly prepared sushi, oysters on the half shell, and other fresh seafood specialties serve to entertain and satisfy the appetite of the patrons of this magnificent brewpub. Brewmaster Eddie Kuehne likens his freshly brewed beer to "getting a fresh, hot loaf of bread right out of the oven versus buying a loaf of bread at the grocery store." Next time you visit Las Vegas, take a stroll down to the Triple 7 Restaurant and Brewery for an evening of tasty beer, good food, and great entertainment.

Tortellini
WITH GORGONZOLA CHIVE SAUCE

You will want to have a basket heaped with crusty bread to sop up the extra sauce.

3 tablespoons butter, divided

1 tablespoon flour

1 cup milk

2 cloves garlic, chopped

1¼ cups Triple 7 Brewery High Roller Gold Ale

¼ cup dry white wine

8 ounces (1 cup) Gorgonzola cheese, crumbled

¼ cup snipped fresh chives

Salt and freshly ground black pepper, to taste

1½ pounds cheese tortellini, cooked in boiling salted water until tender, then drained

1 tomato, finely diced

In a small saucepan, combine 1 tablespoon of the butter and flour and stir with a fork until smooth. Place the saucepan over medium heat until the butter mixture is bubbly. Whisk in the

(continued on next page)

milk in a thin stream until completely incorporated. Cook over medium heat, whisking constantly, until the mixture has slightly thickened. Remove from heat and set aside.

In a large saucepan, melt the remaining 2 tablespoons of butter over medium heat. Add the garlic and sauté until fragrant. Add the ale and wine and simmer until mixture is reduced to 3/4 cup. Reduce heat to medium-low and stir in the reserved milk mixture, Gorgonzola, chives, salt, and pepper until the mixture is smooth. Add the cooked tortellini and simmer until heated through. Pour into a shallow pasta bowl and garnish with the diced tomato.

Serves 4

 **Serve with Triple 7 Brewery High Roller Gold Ale**

Valley Forge Brewing Company

We have all heard stories about the miserable winter spent by General Washington's troops at Valley Forge. The lack of provisions was a daunting hardship for our early freedom fighters. Luckily, no such conditions exist today. Visitors to the Valley Forge Brewing Company's pubs in Wayne and Blue Bell, Pennsylvania, can enjoy a pub experience that combines excellent beers and creative foods in a setting conducive to enjoyment of the heritage of America's freedom. Redcoats are as welcome as our own militia, and both can enjoy tipping a pint and toasting King George of England and the original thirteen free states.

The Baron's Baked Brie

Brie, interestingly enough, was declared the world's finest cheese at the Treaty of Versailles at the conclusion of the First World War.

1 roasted red bell pepper, peeled and chopped

$1/2$ cup chopped cilantro

$1/2$ cup chopped onion

$1/2$ cup roasted garlic

$3/4$ teaspoon freshly ground black pepper

$1/2$ teaspoon minced fresh rosemary

$1/2$ teaspoon salt

8 ounces cream cheese, at room temperature

1 (12-ounce) wheel of Brie

Sourdough bread

Apples and pears, sliced

Preheat oven to 375 degrees F. Lightly oil a pie plate.

In the bowl of a food processor, combine the roasted pepper, cilantro, garlic, onion, pepper, rosemary, and salt and process until smooth. Add the cream cheese and pulse until blended.

Place the Brie in the prepared pie plate. Spread the cream cheese mixture on top of the Brie and bake for about 20 minutes, or until the cream cheese is golden brown and bubbly. Serve hot with the sourdough bread, apple and pear slices.

Serves 8 to 10

Serve with Valley Forge Brewing Company Regiment Pale Ale

Yankee Baked Beans

You can't get much more American than this quintessential recipe!

1 pound great northern white beans,
  thoroughly rinsed

4 cups water

3 cups Valley Forge Brewing Company Regiment
  Pale Ale

1 onion, chopped

2 tablespoons chopped garlic

1 to 2 jalapeño chiles, seeded and chopped

2 cups ketchup

1 cup packed brown sugar

1/2 cup molasses

1/4 cup butter

1/4 cup Dijon mustard

1/4 cup cider vinegar

1 1/2 teaspoons dry mustard

1 teaspoon salt

1/2 teaspoon freshly ground black pepper

1/4 cup butter

 In a large pot, combine the white beans, water, and ale. Cover and let stand overnight.

Preheat oven to 375 degrees F.

Place the pot of beans and their soaking liquid on top of the stove. Bring to a boil over high heat. Reduce heat to medium-low and simmer, uncovered, for $1\frac{1}{2}$ to 2 hours, or until most of the liquid is absorbed.

In the bowl of a food processor, combine the onion, garlic, and chiles and process until smooth. Stir onion mixture into the beans. Stir in ketchup, brown sugar, molasses, butter, Dijon mustard, vinegar, dry mustard, salt, and pepper. Dot with butter. Cover pot and bake the beans for about $1\frac{1}{2}$ hours, or until the mixture is thick and the beans are very tender.

Serves 8

Serve with Valley Forge Brewing Company Regiment Pale Ale

Chipotle and Porter Barbecued Spareribs

The great thing about America's culinary tradition is that it draws on all areas for its ingredients. The southwest flavors of this dish marry with the porter brilliantly.

Chipotle and Porter Barbecue Sauce:

1 cup Valley Forge Brewing Company George's Porter

1 cup ketchup

1/2 cup molasses

1/2 cup yellow mustard

1/4 cup Worcestershire sauce

Juice of one lemon

2 tablespoons canned chipotle in adobo, finely chopped

2 tablespoons chopped garlic

2 tablespoons cider vinegar

1 1/2 teaspoons cayenne

1 1/2 teaspoons chili powder

1 1/2 teaspoons paprika

4 racks pork spareribs

Salt and freshly ground black pepper, to taste

For the sauce: In a saucepan, stir together the beer, ketchup, molasses, mustard, Worcestershire sauce, lemon juice, chipotle in adobo, garlic, vinegar, cayenne, chili powder, and paprika. Bring to a simmer over medium heat. Continue to simmer, stirring often, until thick, about 10 minutes.

Peel off the membrane on the underside of the ribs. Season the ribs with salt and pepper. Prepare a medium-hot charcoal fire. Arrange coals in a ring around the perimeter of the grill and place an aluminum foil pan in the center to catch the dripping fat. Place the ribs, meaty-side up, on the grate. Cover the grill and keep the heat at medium for 2 hours. During the last 45 minutes of cooking, brush the sauce over the ribs several times until all of the sauce is used.

Serves 4

Serve with Valley Forge Brewing Company George's Porter

Honey and Imperial Stout Glazed Salmon

This sweet and savory glaze works beautifully with the rich flavor of the salmon.

2/3 cup Valley Forge Brewing Company
   Imperial Stout

1/2 cup honey

1/2 cup malt vinegar

1/4 cup vegetable oil

2 tablespoons freshly squeezed lime juice

1 1/2 tablespoons chopped fresh parsley

1 1/2 tablespoons chopped fresh tarragon

Salt and freshly ground black pepper, to taste

1 salmon fillet (2 pounds) skinned and
   small bones removed

1 1/2 tablespoons cold butter, cut into small pieces

In a bowl, whisk together the stout, honey, malt vinegar, vegetable oil, lime juice, parsley, tarragon, salt, and pepper until smooth. Pour half of the mixture into a shallow dish large enough to hold the salmon. Place the salmon in the dish, cover, and refrigerate for 8 hours, turning once. Pour the remaining marinade into a small saucepan and simmer over medium heat until the mixture is reduced by half. Remove from heat and whisk in the cold butter until blended. Set aside and keep warm.

Prepare a hot charcoal fire. Remove salmon from the marinade and transfer to the grill. Cook until the fish just flakes. When the salmon is done, place on a platter and pour the sauce over the top.

Serves 6

Serve with Valley Forge Brewing Company Imperial Stout

Irish Lamb Stew

You don't have to wait for St. Paddy's day to enjoy this fine and savory stew.

3 tablespoons vegetable oil

2^1/$_2$ pounds lamb stew meat

1 cup all-purpose flour

^{1}/$_2$ cup tomato paste

1 cup Valley Forge Brewing Company
    George's Porter

2 cups beef stock

3 red potatoes, cut into ^{1}/$_2$-inch cubes

1 carrot, sliced

3 ounces pearl onions, peeled

Salt and freshly ground black pepper, to taste

6 small round loaves sourdough bread

Preheat oven to 350 degrees F.

In a large pot, heat oil over medium-high heat. Dredge the lamb in the flour, shaking off the excess. Add the lamb to the pot and brown well on all sides. Stir in the tomato paste and sauté 1 minute. Stir in the porter, scraping up any browned bits. Stir in the beef stock and bring to a simmer. Cover and place in oven for $1^1/2$ hours. Remove from oven and stir in the potatoes, carrots, onions, salt, and pepper. Cover and bake an additional 30 minutes.

Cut the tops off the bread. Hollow out each loaf leaving a $^1/2$-inch shell. Place the bread on a baking sheet and bake until golden, about 15 minutes.

To serve, place each loaf on a plate and ladle the stew into the hollowed loaf.

Serves 6

 **Serve with Valley Forge Brewing Company George's Porter**

Victory Brewing
Company

Victory. It sounds like a bold statement coming from a small brewery, but then, most of their beers are bold statements. No suits, bean-counters, or marketing stiffs liven the halls of this brewery. Nope, no way, never. Bill Covaleski and Ron Barchet do it all. They still pull on their boots one leg at a time, shovel out a mash tun, wipe down their bar, and serve their beers to lovers of the golden liquid. An abandoned Pepperidge Farm facility serves as their brewpub, and their neighbors in Downingtown, Pennsylvania, have heartily embraced their efforts. Great beer, a dry and warm place to sit, and something tasty for the stomach are the attributes of this eclectic and individual brewpub.

Grilled Swordfish with Spinach, Feta, Tomatoes, and Lemon

If swordfish is unavailable, halibut is a good substitute.

3 tablespoons olive oil

1 pint cherry tomatoes, cut in half

10 cups baby spinach

Juice of 3 lemons

Zest of 3 lemons, finely minced

1 cup crumbled feta cheese

6 (8 ounces each) swordfish steaks

Salt and freshly ground black pepper, to taste

In a large skillet, heat the olive oil over medium heat. Add the cherry tomatoes and sauté until tender. Add the spinach, lemon juice, and lemon zest and sauté until the spinach is wilted and the liquid has almost evaporated. Stir in the feta cheese and heat through. Set aside and keep warm.

(continued on next page)

Prepare a hot grill. Season the swordfish with salt and pepper. Grill the swordfish on both sides until cooked through. Place swordfish steaks on plates and top with spinach mixture.

Serves 6

Serve with Victory Brewing Company Prima Pils

Ale is made of malte and water; and they the whiche do put any other thynge to ale than is rehersed, except yest, barme or godesgood, doth sophysticat theyr ale.

Andrew Boorde's 1542 best-seller,
A Compendious Regyment or a Dyetary of Helth

North African Chicken

This dish is deliciously transformed by the heady spices of Algiers. Some cous cous on the side would be perfect with this chicken, or some fragrant basmati rice.

1 cup all-purpose flour

1 tablespoon curry powder

1 teaspoon cumin

1 teaspoon paprika

3/4 teaspoon turmeric

1/4 teaspoon cayenne

1/4 teaspoon garlic powder

1/4 teaspoon onion powder

1/8 teaspoon saffron

6 split chicken breasts with skin left on

Salt and freshly ground black pepper, to taste

1/4 cup vegetable oil

In a shallow dish, with a fork stir together the flour, curry powder, cumin, paprika, turmeric, cayenne, garlic powder, onion powder,

(continued on next page)

and saffron until well blended. Season the chicken breasts with salt and pepper. Dredge in the flour-spice mixture. In a large skillet, heat the oil over medium-high heat. Place the chicken breasts, skin-side down, in the skillet and brown well. Turn chicken over, reduce heat to medium-low, and continue to cook until chicken is done.

Serves 6

 **Serve with Victory Brewing Company Hop Devil**

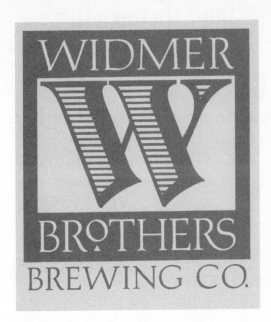

Widmer Brothers
Brewing Company

Best known in the Pacific Northwest for their Hefeweizen, brothers Curt and Rob Widmer literally started out with used dairy tanks and a red pickup truck to deliver their hand-crafted beers to draft accounts in Portland. After some tough times, it wasn't until they decided to keg and market their cloudy-style wheat beer that real success arrived. Now, along with their traditional flagship wheat beer, Widmer bottles and distributes a full range of English and German-style beers. Keep an eye on the future of this pioneer brewery, for Widmer is truly an example of the American rags to riches dream.

Brie and Artichoke Dip

*This is a great party dish that can be
prepared in advance and baked just before
your hungry guests arrive.*

1 pound Brie cheese, diced

12 ounces Swiss cheese, grated

2 cups diced artichoke bottoms (canned,
   packed in brine)

$1^1/2$ cups sour cream

$2/3$ cup heavy cream

$1/3$ cup chopped sun-dried tomatoes

1 teaspoon freshly ground black pepper

1 teaspoon dried red chile flakes

1 teaspoon minced fresh rosemary

French bread

Preheat oven to 350 degrees F. Lightly oil a 1¹/₂-quart baking dish.

In large bowl, stir together the Brie, Swiss cheese, artichokes, sour cream, cream, sun-dried tomatoes, pepper, red chile flakes, and rosemary. Transfer to the prepared baking dish and bake for about 30 minutes, or until top is golden brown and bubbly. Serve with fresh crusty French bread.

Serves 8 to 10

 Serve with Widmer Brothers Brewing Company Hefeweizen

He was a wise man who invented beer.

Plato

Cioppino
WITH HOPJACK PALE ALE

If you have a source for great seafood, then by all means try this cioppino.

1/4 cup olive oil

1 onion, diced

1 tablespoon chopped garlic

2 red bell peppers, diced

1 Anaheim chile, seeded and diced

1 tablespoon marjoram

1 teaspoon dried red chile flakes

1 cup Widmer Brothers Brewing Company
   Hopjack Pale Ale

3 pounds Roma tomatoes, chopped

3 tablespoons minced fresh basil

2 teaspoons salt

1 teaspoon white pepper

1/4 teaspoon saffron

1 1/2 pounds red snapper, cut into 2-inch pieces

1 pound medium shrimp, shelled and deveined

8 ounces scallops

In a large stock-pot, heat the olive oil over medium-high heat. Add the onion and garlic and sauté until tender. Add the bell peppers and Anaheim chile and sauté until tender. Stir in the marjoram and dried red chile flakes. Stir in the ale and bring to a simmer. Stir in tomatoes, basil, salt, white pepper, and saffron and bring to a simmer. Reduce heat to medium-low, cover the pot, and simmer for 30 minutes. Increase heat under pot to medium, and add the red snapper, shrimp, and scallops. Simmer gently until the seafood is cooked through, taking care not to overcook. Ladle into 6 bowls and serve immediately.

Serves 6

Serve with Widmer Brothers Brewing Company Hopjack Pale Ale

Black Bean Soup
with Winternacht Beer

On a cold winter day, nothing warms better than this thick and hearty soup.

1 pound dried black beans

2 tablespoons vegetable oil

2 red bell peppers, diced

1 onion, diced

1 jalapeño chile, minced

2 tablespoons finely chopped garlic

1^1/2 cups Widmer Brothers Brewing Company
  Winternacht Beer

2 tomatoes, chopped

1 can (4 ounces) roasted green chiles, diced

2 tablespoons honey

2 teaspoons chili powder

1 teaspoon cumin

1 teaspoon oregano

5 cups water

1 teaspoon salt

Sour cream, for garnish

Chopped fresh cilantro, for garnish

Rinse the black beans in cold water. Place the beans in a large bowl and cover with plenty of cold water. Let stand overnight. The next day, drain the beans in a colander and set aside.

In a large stock-pot, heat the vegetable oil over medium heat. Add the bell peppers, onion, and jalapeño and sauté until tender. Stir in the garlic and sauté until fragrant. Add the beer and bring to a simmer. Stir in the tomatoes, green chiles, honey, chili powder, cumin, oregano, water, and the reserved black beans and bring to a simmer. Reduce heat to medium-low, cover the pot, and simmer for about 1 hour, or until the beans are tender. Remove the lid and stir in salt. Simmer until the soup is thick. Place half of the soup in a blender and purée until smooth. Return the soup to the pot and heat through. Serve in bowls with dollops of sour cream and a sprinkle of cilantro.

Serves 6 to 8

Serve with Widmer Brothers Brewing Company Winternacht Beer

Breweries

Alaskan Brewing Co.
5429 Shane Drive
Juneau, AK 99801
907.780.5866

Anchor Brewing Co.
1705 Mariposa Street
San Francisco, CA 94107
415.863.8350

Anderson Valley Brewing Co.
14081 Highway 128
Boonville, CA 95415
800.207.BEER

Bear Republic Brewing Co.
345 Healdsburg Avenue
Healdsburg, CA 95448
707.433.BEER

Beerman's Beerwerks and
    Meat Market
645 Fifth Street
Lincoln, CA 95648
916.645.2377

B J's Restaurant and Brewery
16162 Beach Boulevard,
    Suite 100
Hunting Beach, CA 92647
714.848.3747

Boston Beer Works
61 Brookline Avenue
Boston, MA 02215
617.536.BEER

Deschutes Brewery
1044 N.W. Bond Street
Bend, OR 97701
541.382.9242

Full Sail Brewing Co.
506 Columbia Street
Hood River, OR 97031
541.386.2281

Golden Pacific Brewing Co.
1404 Fourth Street
Berkeley, CA 94710
510.558.1919

Great Divide Brewing Co.
2201 Arapahoe Street
Denver, CO 80205
303.296.9460

Harbor Public House
231 Parfitt Way S.W.
Bainbridge Island, WA 98110
206.842.0969

Iron Hill Brewery and
    Restaurant
30 East State Street
Media, PA 19063
610.627.9000

Lost Coast Brewery
123 West Third Street
Eureka, CA 95501
707.445.4484

McGuire's Pub
600 East Gregory Street
Pensacola, FL 32501
850.433.6789

Mount St. Helena Brewing Co.
21167 Calistoga Street
Middletown, CA 95461
707.987.3361

North Coast Brewing Co.
444 North Main Street
Fort Bragg, CA 95437
707.964.BREW

Pennsylvania Brewing Co.
800 Vinial Street
Pittsburgh, PA 15212
412.237.9400

Pizza Port
135 North Highway 101
Solano Beach, CA 92075
619.481.7332

Prescott Brewing Co.
130 West Gurley Street, Ste. A
Prescott, AZ 86301
520.771.2795

Pyramid Brewery
1201 First Avenue South
Seattle, WA 98134
206.682.3377

Rock Bottom Restaurants
248 Centennial Parkway,
    Suite 100
Louisville, CO 80027
303.664.4000

Rockies Brewing Co.
2880 Wilderness Place
Boulder, CO 80301
303.444.8448

Rogue Ales
2320 OSU Drive
Newport, OR 97365
541.867.3660

Russian River Brewing Co.
13250 River Road
Guerneville, CA 95446
707.824.7000

Sierra Nevada Brewing Co.
1075 East 20th Street
Chico, CA 95928
530.893.3520

Silverado Brewing Co.
3020 North St. Helena
    Highway
St. Helena, CA 94574
707.967.9876

South Hampton Public House
40 Bowden Square
Southhampton, NY 11968
516.283.2800

Stoudt Brewing Co.
Route 272
Adamstown, PA 19501
717.484.4386

Titanic Brewing Co.
5813 Ponce de Leon Blvd.
Coral Gables, FL 33146
305.667.ALES

Trap Rock Brewery
279 Springfield Heights
Berkeley Heights, NJ 07922
908.665.1755

Triple 7 Restaurant & Brewery
200 North Main Street
Las Vegas, NV 89101
702.387.1896

Valley Forge Brewing Co.
799 Dekalb Pike
Blue Bell, PA 19422
610.279.4700

Victory Brewing Co.
420 Acorn Lane
Downington, PA 19335
610.873.0881

Widmer Bros. Brewing Co.
929 North Russell
Portland, OR 97227
503.281.BIER

Also by Leslie Mansfield

Recipes from the Vineyards of Northern California

An accomplished chef and long-time Napa Valley resident, Leslie Mansfield has gathered signature recipes from more than fifty of Napa and Sonoma Countys' world-class wineries. Each flavorful dish is accompanied by a suggested wine selection. So, relax and let the winemakers of California's true "gold country" do the cooking and experience the unparalleled pleasure of eating spectacular food served with the perfect glass of wine.

Appetizers $9.95 ISBN 0-89087-890-0

Main Courses $9.95 ISBN 0-89087-891-9

Desserts $9.95 ISBN 0-89087-892-7

Barbecue $9.95 ISBN 0-89087-958-3

Picnics $9.95 ISBN 0-89087-960-5

Vegetarian Dishes $9.95 ISBN 0-89087-959-1

Pasta with Red Wine $9.95 ISBN 0-89087-936-2

Pasta with White Wine $9.95 ISBN 0-89087-937-0

Asian Pasta $9.95 ISBN 0-89087-938-9

To order call toll free (800) 841-BOOK

For more information on other Celestial Arts titles,
log on to our website at **www.tenspeed.com**

Conversions

Liquid

1 tablespoon = 15 milliliters

$1/2$ cup = 4 fluid ounces = 125 milliliters

1 cup = 8 fluid ounces = 250 milliliters

Dry

$1/4$ cup = 4 tablespoons = 2 ounces = 60 grams

1 cup = $1/2$ pound = 8 ounces = 250 grams

Flour

$1/2$ cup = 60 grams

1 cup = 4 ounces = 125 grams

Temperature

400 degrees F = 200 degrees C = gas mark 6

375 degrees F = 190 degrees C = gas mark 5

350 degrees F = 175 degrees C = gas mark 4

Miscellaneous

2 tablespoons butter = 1 ounce = 30 grams